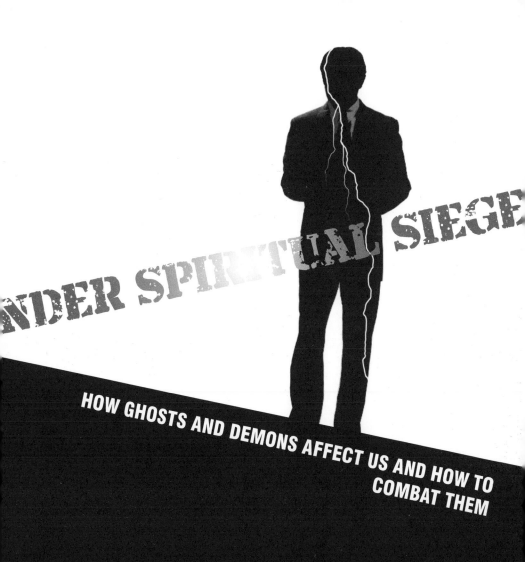

UNDER SPIRITUAL SIEGE

HOW GHOSTS AND DEMONS AFFECT US AND HOW TO COMBAT THEM

WILLIAM STILLMAN

Schiffer Publishing Ltd

4880 Lower Valley Road • Atglen, PA 19310

Library of Congress Control Number: 2016931567

Designed by RoS
Cover design by Brenda McCallum
Type set in Armalite Rifle/NewBskvll BT

ISBN: 978-0-7643-5042-9
Printed in China

Published by Schiffer Publishing, Ltd.
4880 Lower Valley Road
Atglen, PA 19310
Phone: (610) 593-1777; Fax: (610) 593-2002
E-mail: Info@schifferbooks.com

For our complete selection of fine books on this and related subjects, please visit our website at www.schifferbooks.com. You may also write for a free catalog.

This book may be purchased from the publisher.

We are always looking for people to write books on new and related subjects. If you have an idea for a book, please contact us at proposals@schifferbooks.com.

Schiffer Publishing's titles are available at special discounts for bulk purchases for sales promotions or premiums. Special editions, including personalized covers, corporate imprints, and excerpts, can be created in large quantities for special needs. For more information, contact the publisher.

Cover images: Spotlight Black and White Lighting Equipment © molodec. Zombie Apocalypse © _Lonely_. Courtesy www.bigstockphoto.com

DEDICATION

**This book is dedicated to any young person
who is enduring dark times,
as I once did.
Have faith in your faith.**

As someone who directs a professional paranormal resolution team, I believe William Stillman has perfectly captured the essence of what so many of our clients go through. Through sharing personal life experiences with an understanding of the spirit world, William details the often misunderstood and seldom realized interconnectedness between the living and spirit world that creates unique and sometimes unpleasant situations for all involved. William offers brilliant advice on how to understand and deal with a variety of spiritual issues, encouraging the reader to empower and heal themselves and others through love and compassion, the strongest weapons in the fight against darkness. This book is sure to be a recommended resource for all of our clients dealing with paranormal and spiritual issues.

—Mark A. Keyes
Director of The Pennsylvania Paranormal Association and author of *Chasing Shadows: A Criminal Investigator's Look into the Paranormal*

William Stillman escorts the reader on a guided tour through his many experiences in the paranormal realm in a way that only a person with his unique qualifications can deliver. Diversely interesting, reflective, and educational.

—Don Traynor
Founder, Village Haunts Paranormal History Experiences, Bemus Point, New York

This book is a must for anyone going through times of spiritual change. You will recognize yourself throughout and find answers to the questions you've been seeking. I highly recommend *Under Spiritual Siege* to anyone experiencing a spiritual awakening, whether it be in the light or in the dark. Here's your guidebook.

—Carol Mills
Psychic Medium

Under Spiritual Siege empowers spiritual seekers with the practical tools to engage, connect, and communicate with our spirit guides. Stillman's firsthand accounts of his experiences with the spirit world will have you riveted to your seat. A "must read" for anyone on a spiritual path!

—Mary Riposo, PhD
Reiki Master Teacher and co-owner of Infinite Light Center for Yoga & Wellness

Under Spiritual Siege is a must-have guide for anyone interested in navigating the integral phase of human consciousness with ease and grace. I plan to refer to it often.

—Kathleen McManis
Author, *Being Beautiful through Energy and Love* and founder of AlternativeSkin

Under Spiritual Siege is a comprehensive look at the very real world of ghosts and demons, and the toll they can take on us—mentally, physically and spiritually. It also gives you important information so you can both understand that impact, as well as protect yourself and those you love.

—Ken Kessler
Host of *Psychic Tapestry* radio show

CONTENTS

INTRODUCTION

Are ghosts and demons real? Is it possible for these entities to have an effect on our mental, physical, and spiritual well-being? The answer to both questions is a resounding "yes!" I have had up-close-and-personal interaction with both types of energies, and I can tell you without a doubt that their negativity can affect our overall health as well as our relationships in ways that are counterproductive at best and destructive at worst. The most damaging of these issues can include the sensation of intrusive thoughts instructing one to harm oneself and others.

The degree to which these negative energies can affect all aspects of our lives has been grossly underestimated or written off as New Age foolishness, religious fantasy, or mental illness. The irony is that these conclusions are precisely what the negative energies wish for us to believe in order to continue their campaign of chaos and destruction. It is spiritual warfare and a form of bullying on a whole new level. However, in your hands you hold a remedy: a book to grant you knowledge and wisdom to learn not only how to protect yourself and others, but how to join forces with other like-minded visionaries to conquer nefarious entities.

Under Spiritual Siege: How Ghosts and Demons Affect Us and How to Combat Them will be your handbook for knowing how to discern ghosts and demons and to distinguish the difference between them. You will understand that you are protected by spiritual allies and cheerleaders, and you'll learn how they can communicate with you. You will also be instructed how to help others who are struggling with spiritual assault, such as clearing a home of negative energy. Finally, you will be empowered to participate in becoming the antidote to counteract a spiritual siege that is slowly but steadily increasing as our world becomes divided into two factions: those who are narcissistic, insensitive, and callous, and those who are kind, compassion, and altruistic.

More than ever, it is urgent that you enlist in the faction that can rectify the change for a season of peace, tranquility, and brotherhood. It is overdue and time is of the essence.

Chapter One
PSYCHIC ME

First off you should know this: I'm a psychic. But then, I believe we are *all* psychic. Psychic gifts manifest differently in each person. That's the neat thing about being diverse human beings: your gifts are as unique as your DNA. One of my psychic gifts is that I am *clairvoyant*, which is French for "clear seeing." I get fragments of pictures and movies in my head, sort of like shaking up the Magic 8-Ball and waiting for the message to rise to the surface through the inky liquid. Another way to think of it is like when you are able to visually catch some of the fleeting news ticker at the bottom of the TV screen on a news station. Sometimes I'll also see a word paired with an image or I'll see the first initial of someone's name. This all happens in my mind's eye; I'm not literally seeing something floating in the air. When I am in contact with the spirit of someone who has passed on, it's not like I'm carrying on a complete conversation. I'm shown bits and pieces of visual information that I then translate into words. It's called telepathy, a silent process of mental exchange. This doesn't happen to me constantly, 24/7. In order to put on my psychic "hat," I deliberately get into that "zone" by protecting myself with a prayer and then meditating for about a half hour or so.

The first thing you should know about being psychic yourself is that it's your birthright as a human being. The second thing is that you should not be turned "on" 24/7—no one is, no matter how it appears on psychic or ghost hunter TV shows. Being "on" all the time will drain you of your physical, mental-emotional, and spiritual well-being. It will also disempower you from saying "no" to any negative force that wishes to cause you to become derailed or undone. (More about caring for yourself properly in chapters six and eight.)

I have been working as a psychic professionally since 2004, providing private one-on-one psychic readings. What many people don't understand about psychics, and why we're not always spot-on, is that I can only "see" and be shown what I would know to recognize and understand because I've lived it or I've experienced it myself. The challenge is that you have lived an entirely different life from me, so while we will have *some* experiences in common, many others will require some finessing to appreciate. For example, I am a homebody and have no interest in traveling, especially to other countries. You, on the other hand, may love to travel and of all the places you've been, Paris, France, could be your favorite destination. I've never been to Paris so my point of reference is limited to the French I took in high school or possibly an image of the Eiffel Tower. So, instead, in a psychic reading for you, I may receive the impression of Pepé le Pew, the lovesick French skunk from Looney Tunes cartoons! Now my task is to decipher what I'm intended to convey: Is this an indication that you have, or had, a pet skunk? Are you interested in vintage animation? Or, is this a reference to France? So you can appreciate how even the most skilled psychic may require some support to tweak the information so that it makes sense for each client.

Over the years, I've learned to say what I see when I'm receiving the pictures and movies in my mind, no matter how far-out it may sound. Usually, through the grace of God, what I see is in the ballpark in terms of accuracy, even though it may make no sense at the time. For example, I was once giving a psychic reading to a client who was close to her deceased grandmother. For some odd reason, I kept getting the impression of a turtle. My job as a psychic is to be an interpreter between two worlds, kind of like translating a foreign language—in which I'm somewhat fluent—for someone who doesn't speak the language at all. It can be a challenging task because, as

UNDER SPIRITUAL SIEGE

I've indicated, the spiritual communications I receive are rather cryptic images, symbols, or icons. In the case of the turtle, neither I nor my client understood how to interpret it, so I set it aside and moved on to discussing other topics. A short while afterwards, my client contacted me to say she had been to the cemetery to place flowers on her grandmother's grave. On the headstone had been placed a small green-glass turtle! She has no idea how it got there or why, but she accepted it as a validation from her psychic reading.

In addition to psychic readings, I also conduct psychic galleries. The galleries are much the same as those group readings conducted by John Edward on the TV show *Crossing Over*. That is, after having prayed and meditated privately, I say a prayer with a roomful of people who have gathered together in order to protect and "ground" the group. I next allow God to guide me to receive the intuitive impressions that I am entrusted to communicate. It's a strange and curious process, and certainly never dull! Oftentimes, I'm shown some random tidbit of an audience member's life as the means of singling out him or her. Oftentimes, the random tidbit has nothing to do with the message to be delivered. For example, during a recent gallery I was shown the image of the entertainer Barry Manilow, so I asked, "Who's the Barry Manilow fan?" Two hands shot up in the air, so I had to narrow it down. I was then shown Barry Manilow in concert, so I asked, "Which of you has seen him in concert?" and only one hand remained up. I was then able to focus my attention on this person and deliver a message that had nothing to do with Barry Manilow! (Oddly enough, the two people who were both his fans sat in the same row, one person apart, and didn't know one another.)

In another instance, I felt that the forthcoming communication was intended for one of the gentlemen in the room. I saw that a father figure bought him Tonka Trucks as a boy (I was very clearly shown the word TONKA) and that a grandfather had a baseball connection, whether it was attending games or collecting baseball cards. No one was claiming the information until finally an older man spoke up to say that his dad did get him Tonka Trucks to play with as a boy. When I asked about a baseball connection to his father's father, the man seemed hesitant until he finally recalled that his grandfather, a carpenter, used to *make* baseball bats for the local high school!

So you see, the iconography of Spiritspeak is like an ethereal version of charades for advanced players. Here are some common symbols regularly communicated to me:

- ◈ SWOLLEN ANKLES = DIABETES
- ◈ ARM'S LENGTH = EMOTIONAL AND/OR GEOGRAPHIC DISTANCE
- ◈ SALUTE = MILITARY OR OFFICIAL, UNIFORMED SERVICE
- ◈ EXPOSED INNER ARM = ANYTHING HARDER THAN MARIJUANA
- ◈ GAS STOVE WITH BURNER LEFT ON = ALZHEIMER'S/DEMENTIA
- ◈ ROSES = SPIRITUAL COMMUNICATION ACKNOWLEDGING A CELEBRATION (BIRTHDAY, ANNIVERSARY, OR ACHIEVEMENT)
- ◈ HOWDY DOODY = REASONABLY HAPPY AND CAREFREE CHILDHOOD
- ◈ BIRDS OR NUMBERS IN PATTERNS OF THREE = SPIRITUAL COMMUNICATION
- ◈ TWO RAMS BUTTING HEADS = STUBBORN RELATIONSHIP, USUALLY WITH A FAMILY MEMBER
- ◈ FRANK SINATRA SINGING "I DID IT MY WAY" = A FIERCELY WILLFUL, INDEPENDENT PERSONALITY
- ◈ A TOUGH COOKIE (UNABLE TO BITE IT) = STRONG, RESILIENT PERSONALITY
- ◈ BASKETBALL SCOREBOARD = ACCRUING SPIRITUAL POINTS FOR SELFLESS AND COMPASSIONATE WORK
- ◈ SPINNING TIRE IN MUD = STUCK, STAGNANT IN JOB OR RELATIONSHIP
- ◈ THREE-FOOT LONG BLACK LEECHES HANGING OFF CLIENT = NEGATIVE SPIRITUAL ATTACHMENT
- ◈ KIDS WITHOUT HAIR = AFFILIATION WITH, OR THE NEED TO ALIGN WITH, A CHILDREN'S CHARITY
- ◈ TV WITH MILTON BERLE = SENSE OF HUMOR, WANTS TO BE REMEMBERED FOR SUCH
- ◈ COLUMN OF GOLDEN LIGHT = ANGEL
- ◈ BIRTHDAY CAKE = BIRTHDAY OR FAMILY CELEBRATION, SUCH AS A REUNION
- ◈ SHIP = TRIP OR VACATION
- ◈ MALE OR FEMALE STANDING DIRECTLY BEHIND CLIENT = SPIRIT GUIDE

This may all sound exciting or cool, but it wasn't always this way. In order for you to accept me as a credible guide, and to believe what I'll be sharing with you in this book, I have to earn your trust. Allow me to give you some background about myself. In so doing, I will anticipate honoring any trust you may place in me by being as honest and transparent as possible, seeking only to illuminate the truth. Here is my story.

MY STORY

I was an exquisitely sensitive little boy. One of my earliest recollections of just *how* sensitive is the time I was sitting in a church pew at five years of age. I was sobbing and couldn't seem to gain control of my emotions. I could tell my parents were becoming restless about my disruption, and they finally took me out and we went home. I had a good reason for crying, I just never told anyone why. I had been staring at a glorious, terrible stained glass window of the crucifixion and openly grieving the pain that Jesus must have endured. One who possesses the ability to internalize the pain and suffering of others as one's own pain is called an *empath*, from the words *empathy* or *empathetic*. This trait is a special form of compassion that we all share innately; but it is slipping away from us as spiritual warfare erodes our sensitivity toward others.

Around this time I recall having strange dreams that sometimes came true. Twice I had a dream in which I picked up pennies that were scattered on our front lawn, only to do so in real life the next day! I have no idea how they got there and why they would be so randomly scattered. Other dreams were more like nightmares, including one that could've been straight out of *The Lord of the Rings* in which I was being pursued by a nasty little troll who hid a piece of parchment with a powerful spell written on it in the empty socket of his toothless gums. Just as he reached me at the top of the attic staircase, I quickly called out magic words, "In the mouth, down the stairs!" at which this Rumpelstiltskin-like character was instantly sent crashing to his death at the bottom of the stairs. It is still a vivid memory decades afterwards.

When I was six, in 1969, we moved to an old house in Pennsylvania. When I was a little older, I learned that one of the former owners had committed suicide by hanging himself in the garage. My father was once working in a dark back room of our basement, and getting up, set down a large, utility-style flashlight only to discover it missing upon his return a few minutes later (it never did turn up, even when packing to move years later). It was also in this house that I spent the worst years of my life.

By the fourth grade, my sensitivity was showing in more obvious ways. I was introverted and usually connected socially only by talking about things that were interesting to me. So much about the world seemed strange to me and I didn't understand a lot of the rules and rationales of most adults. From our front porch I could see the high school I would one day attend in the distance on a hilltop. As a child,

I worried about how I'd ever know how to catch the bus to get there even though that was years in the future. But then I worried about a lot of things, always seeming to experience anxiety over circumstances beyond my control. I, myself, became controlling in compensation, exerting authority unreasonably over three younger brothers.

I must've been seen by my school peers as odd or unusual too—a nerd before the word was even in widespread use. I wasn't physically coordinated enough for kick ball or other team sports. Once, I became so disoriented that during a gym class game of touch football, I ran in the other direction and scored points for the opposing team.

I didn't have close friends. I was considered hypersensitive, moody, irritable, antisocial, cold, arrogant and aloof. I also became the butt of bullying. For many years, on virtually a daily basis, I was verbally abused, physically harassed, and my speech and body language were publicly mocked and mimicked in front of school bus drivers, cafeteria staff, and teachers who did nothing to intervene. The insensitive person would define these experiences as "part of growing up," and might advise me to "grow a thick skin." But when you are highly sensitive, the world hurts—even bright lights, loud noises, and scratchy clothing. I descended into a dark time.

Instead of finding faith in my faith and holding fast to the empathetic little boy who mourned for Jesus Christ in a church pew, I retreated inward. I became insensitive and cynical. I became cold and hard and gray and ugly, or so I felt. And I became intrigued with dark things. I became preoccupied with movies like *The Exorcist* and *Psycho*. I drew bloody, graphic pictures of the shark from *Jaws* mangling hapless swimmers. I was drawn to pornography, which in the 1970s was pretty tame compared to now. I also became drawn to learn and read about what was then called "the occult": werewolves, vampires, ghosts, demons, witchcraft, and the notion that one could attain supernatural powers to manipulate others. I sent away for mail order catalogs that sold candles, devices, and tools used in casting spells. And though I never purchased anything, I imagined I *did* have abilities that made me "special" and set me above my peers.

At this time, a red, irregularly shaped mark appeared in the center of my right palm. (As an adult, I was stunned to learn that such a mark in one's palm is referenced in the Book of Revelation in the Bible.) It was also then that I began to receive nightly visits from "the dark man." (I will discuss this in detail in chapter four).

My personality became increasingly sullen. The thought of going to school made me queasy and I developed what I now realize was post-traumatic stress disorder. I became severely depressed and contemplated suicide on a regular basis. On one occasion, when I was sixteen, my family went on a day trip and I, preferring to be alone, stayed home. I spent a long time sitting with my father's straight razor and thinking about slashing my wrists. I imagined that after cutting into my flesh, I might panic at first, but that soon enough I'd hear a ringing in my ears that would fill my head completely as I slipped away. But just then, I felt a voice within me say, "No, no, don't do this thing. One day people will know who you are for what it is you have to offer them." I had no idea what that meant or even what that would look like, but it was enough to persuade me to wait it out a little while longer.

I made it through high school and commuted to college (after living on campus my first semester) so that I wouldn't have to deal with the social pressures of dorm life. As I grew and matured into adulthood, I began to recognize that there were occasions in which I felt protected. I had never been in a serious accident, no broken bones, no serious illnesses, and no surgeries. I also always seemed to have money when I needed it; it may have come in the eleventh hour, but I was always "saved" financially. I came to appreciate that my good fortune was extremely unusual. When I was in my mid-thirties, I decided to make a change and honor the source of the protection.

For most of my life up until that time, I had an attitude. I don't think I was a mean person, but I was sarcastic and often said things that were interpreted by others as uncaring. I didn't want to be like that any longer, I wanted to be a better person. I still retained an interest in all things paranormal and in ghosts and psychics; but I began to read books that were about *spirituality*. I came to understand that when one embraces spirituality and surrenders a bitter façade, that paranormal becomes normal and supernatural is natural. I finally realized that I could, indeed, possess the "powers" I had always wanted but with the exception of acknowledging that the source of those abilities originated in God, and that the purpose of them was to serve others selflessly. It was a moment of illumination, an *aha!* moment.

I made a conscious decision to transform myself. I read about a hundred books in a year, spoke about others in kinder ways, and began to pray. Every day. It was something I hadn't done since saying bedtime prayers as a child. Engaging with God as an adult in that daily one-on-one time was a moment of truth because there's no ignoring it and there's no hiding secrets of any kind. It was a time to come clean but also a time to express thanks. Do you remember Dr. Seuss's *The Grinch Who Stole Christmas*? At the end, the Grinch experiences a transformation for realizing that he couldn't steal the spiritual essence of Christmas from the Whos. He changed, and his heart grew several times its original size. That's how I felt. I wasn't permanently locked into portraying myself the way others had come to know me; my behavior was a *choice*. I became kinder, gentler, softer. And I welcomed it.

One of the most significant things I did at this time was to formally acknowledge the protective presence I had always sensed around me. I had read about the concept of *spirit guides* (which I'll discuss in greater detail in chapter six). We all have spirit guides, and they essentially desire to work with us to manifest our spiritual potential, sort of like a psychic version of having Jiminy Cricket helping you to navigate life circumstances. I decided my guide's name was Frank—a name that just popped into my head—and in a prayer, I christened him as such. I knew from reading spiritual books that I should expect a "sign" from my spirit guide about a week to ten days out, which is exactly what happened.

A week after I named Frank, there was a knock on my door. It was the young man driving the garbage truck for that day's pickup. He came to tell me that he split my mailbox post while backing the truck out of my cul-de-sac. I asked if the sanitation company would pay for a replacement and he said they would. But when he handed me the information, I noticed it was *his* name and contact information. Then it dawned on me, and I said, "If I report this, does that put you in any jeopardy?" The young man said it could affect his driving record if I called his boss, and he'd just as soon pay for the replacement post and install the new one himself. I told him I'd think about it and he left.

Within the hour, I decided I would honor his honesty and allow him to take care of it as he had offered (and without reporting it to the company). I went to look at his information on the scrap of paper he had given me. Not only was his name Frank, his last name was Ward. That stuck with me until I looked it up; the definition of the word "ward" pertains to guardianship and the act of keeping guard. This young fella's name translated to "Frank the Guardian!" Now, he was not my guide, it's what he *symbolized* that was the intended communication. (By the way, Frank Ward made good on his promise and when he came back to replace my mailbox post, he told me he wasn't supposed to have been there that day. He was filling in for someone who had called off; it was his first time in the area and his regular driving route was way across the other side of town.)

Once I received this validation, *everything* shot through the roof and I literally made up for decades in about three months! I began to recognize the synchronicities that abounded each day, those fleeting moments when what I'm thinking, reading, or saying lines up precisely with something directly connected in that very second. For example, reading the word "humanitarian" at the same time someone says that very word on television. I also began having what seemed like nightly dreams in which I was being "mentored" by my guide to solve problems or understand certain aspects of humanity. It was then that my intuition became heightened.

Increasingly, I felt pulled to act upon my spiritual growth by doing something more, something greater. I was discontented with my full-time job and yet uncertain of the risks associated with striking out on my own, independently and self-employed. Home alone one day, I decided to ask God for guidance. I said a prayer and requested that the path I should take be indicated to me in a dream. I lay down to take a nap and…nothing happened! But that was *my* time, not *God's* time. That night, after I had forgotten about my prayer, I was awakened shortly after 2:00 a.m. with the sensation of electricity running up and down the length of my body, which is something I'd never experienced before or since. I had just had a profound dream with symbolic imagery that included a white, winged horse (representing my ability to soar). I also awoke with an inner knowing that I could quit my job and everything would be okay, so long as I stayed focused on the truth. The next day, I gave notice at work and walked away from a salaried position with benefits and stepped into the unknown, with nothing else lined up. But I knew I wasn't alone. I would be okay, and I have been ever since.

Now, in hindsight, taking this route was rather drastic and it's not something I endorse, especially for people who have children and are working to support their families—you have to pay the bills! But, for me, at that moment, it was the right decision and I am forever grateful for where my life has taken me. It was also then that I began to further explore my psychic gifts.

I had left my job in 2000 and was making ends meet by freelancing as a consultant to families of children with autism and the agencies that served them. I also began slowly practicing my intuition with others who were open to it. There's lots of ways that a person can do this, but I was never interested in learning how to use Tarot or angel cards, or pendulums or crystals; instead, I wanted to work without devices. After saying a prayer with each person—an important necessity, as you will learn—I focused on any pictures or movies I could see in my mind's eye. It also helped if I held the person's hand in my own. At first, I drew what I was seeing; most of it was symbolic but usually relevant for the person. Later, I discarded the idea of drawing and just verbally communicated what I was seeing. My accuracy rate was encouraging, and I wondered if I could do psychic readings professionally.

I began to survey businesses in my general locale that might entertain the notion of hosting a psychic reader. I live in a fairly conservative area, so there aren't many businesses that specialize in holistic practices. However, after striking out with one or two other places, I found Alta View Wellness Center. Sharon, the owner, agreed to meet me on the condition that I give her a psychic reading, which was not an unreasonable request. She was somewhat ambivalent, though, because she'd had a psychic reader there previously and things hadn't worked out. On the day of the appointment, I went in and had a chat with Sharon, telling her I was looking for a place to call "home." I gave her a reading and I could tell she wasn't exactly blown away, but she later told me she had a specific agenda: she was hoping to hear from her mother who had passed on. Later, when she processed the images I'd shared with her, she realized that much of it made sense. She called me to tell me she was going to give me a chance. That was in 2004, and I have been there ever since.

I love the work that I do. I know it has brought healing and closure for many people. But as I delved into my psychic side, I began to encounter situations in which certain individuals, or their loved ones, were grappling with dark things in the manner that I once had. Enduring those tough times was unpleasant, but I am also thankful for having experienced them. That knowledge and understanding would empower me for even darker things that awaited.

Chapter Two

HOW SPIRIT COMMUNICATES

In order for you to understand the several chapters succeeding this one that deal with insidious and unwelcome presences, it will be helpful for you to recognize how it is that benevolent spirits communicate. These are presences that have successfully transitioned to the Heavenly realm and are precisely where they should be. Many people whom I have encountered don't fully understand the sanctity of Heaven. The soul energies that exist there do so in a blissful state. And while they generally retain aspects of their personalities (or at least project aspects of those personalities in ways others would readily recognize), they do not harbor any resentments or ill will *whatsoever*. In fact, when I am interpreting or *channeling* a loved one in spirit who had a falling out with a family member, they have consistently provided assurances that any past arguments have absolutely no significance any longer. I have seen this occur many times when family members have had a blowout just prior to someone's death. It creates a lot of guilt for the survivors and communicating that all is forgiven relieves a great burden. In Heaven, there exists only high-vibration, high-energy emotions, which are thoughts and feelings such as joy, happiness, the sensation of camaraderie, and, of course, unconditional love. (But Heaven is not all about idly floating on a cloud and eating bonbons!)

This concept is particularly challenging to communicate to families of missing persons or homicide victims. They are grieving a loss and want closure, but their loved one is in a state of total bliss. Locating the cumbersome, heavy, low-energy physical body that once housed their soul or bringing their perpetrator to justice is not their agenda—it's *our* agenda. From their vantage point, they have 360-degree vision; they see the big picture and they understand how their passing succinctly fits into it, while we are still left puzzled and mourning. And so in communicating with those spirits, I frame my requests in the context of what their family requires to attain emotional peace and closure. That sometimes helps.

In one instance, I was tasked with providing any possible insight into the disappearance of Krissie who had vanished from her apartment in the middle of the night, leaving behind her cell phone, purse, and beloved dog. In meeting with her family, I was able to connect with her energy and channel her personality. (I never once said whether I believed she was living or deceased, although I personally believed she had been murdered; and I encouraged the family to take a proactive stance in holding out hope.) But when I began to "ask" Krissie specifics of what became of her, she put a "wall" up in front of me, crossed her arms, and communicated firmly, "No, it's not done yet." What she meant by this was that, spiritually, her circumstances were preordained—believe it or not. In fact, at one point, Krissie—through me—said very matter-of-factly and almost casually, "I wasn't supposed to be here that long anyway." This caused her mother to gasp and say, "She's been telling me that ever since she was a little girl!" Krissie was more concerned with the good things her disappearance had brought out in others and in her community that had rallied in support of her family. She was very confident (to the point of being stubborn, which she was indeed in life) that everyone would learn from her tragic absence—even her perpetrators.

When I first encountered Krissie, in a psychic sense, she was dancing and twirling in a flowery meadow I have since come to learn is called *Summerland*. I had seen this place once before, in a dream. It was a very vivid dream in which I found myself on the outskirts of what I understood to be Heaven. It was a gorgeous wooded area with a beautiful meadow of green grass dotted with daisies. There was also a mesmerizing waterfall that butted up against what looked like a large music auditorium (I wasn't able to go beyond this point).

UNDER SPIRITUAL SIEGE

What I recall most about this dream experience is that all of my senses were heightened. I could inhale the wonderful pine aroma of the trees more than I normally could, and I felt as though I was one with the cascading waterfall just by looking at it. This dream was an enticing glimpse of the place of transition between Heaven and earth.

In fact, dreams are one of the more common ways in which spirit communicates with us. It is a "safe" way to reach us because it occurs in a surreal state instead of playing out before us in real time, which could be extremely unsettling for many people. But since infancy, we've been conditioned to accept that in dreams the absurd is plausible and anything can happen, logically or otherwise. Because we are asleep and our minds are relaxed and undistracted, the dream becomes the vehicle by which we are a captive audience and spirit can reach us most effectively. Have you ever had a dream in which you were reunited with a loved one who had died? It should have been a joyful, pleasant experience. You probably communicated with him or her without remembering that either of you actually spoke by moving your mouth. This person may have looked much younger and healthier, but you still recognized them. And you may have awakened from the dream weeping because the experience was bittersweet. If the dream was particularly vivid and met these criteria, it is called *a visitation*. And it is as real as you can come in human form to the kind of reunion that will occur once you reach Heaven.

Another way in which our loved ones in spirit communicate with us is through the manipulation of certain creatures, birds, and insects. (You'll read in the next chapter of my unexpected encounter with a lone fawn.) Most often, we would associate the unexpected appearance of these creatures with memories we have of a specific person. For example, one client talked of how a unique bird with a call that sounded like "purdy, purdy, purdy" appeared within twenty-four hours of her birthday; it reminded her of her mother and how her mom always used to say, "Pretty, pretty, pretty." It was comforting to my client and an appropriate way for her to interpret this interesting coincidence. In another instance, I had breakfast with a friend during which she shared her spiritual connection to hawks, and how she perceived them as "signs." She told one story in particular about needing a sign while a passenger in a car, and a large hawk swooped right next to her window. On the drive home from meeting with her, I was thinking about this and, in that very moment, a hawk soared across the road in front of my car.

Common creatures that are spiritual calling cards tend to be butterflies, which are beautiful to look at and symbolize the ability of flight; bright red cardinals, whose striking color signifies the vibrancy of life-blood; and ladybugs, which symbolize releasing worry and frustration and trusting in God. Once, as I came out of the post office, I noticed that the license plate on the truck parked next to my car said, "3 LBUG," and the license plate frame was decorated with ladybugs. As I stood there, a woman said, "Do you agree with that?" thinking I was looking at her "Yankees Suck!" bumper sticker. I asked if her license plate referred to ladybugs, and she said she calls her three nieces her three little ladybugs and buys them ladybug items.

The unexpected appearance of such a creature may be magnified if it is not typically indigenous to your area, such as spotting an uncommon butterfly that is native to Texas and you live in Maine! And just to be clear: your loved one is *not* the reincarnation of a butterfly nor is your loved one a bird in cardinal form. But, if the timing of such a creature's appearance seems profound, your loved one has likely impressed spiritual inspiration within the creature, causing it to be present at just the proper moment so that it resonates with you.

Finding coins unexpectedly or in strikingly coincidental locations is in keeping with the idea of "pennies from Heaven" as another manner in which a loving spiritual presence communicates. (I recall my childhood dreams on two occasions of finding pennies on the front lawn and, upon awakening, actually had it happen!) Sometimes it's a solitary and specific coin that we would connect in our fond thoughts of a special someone who has passed on: for example, if your grandma always said, "Penny for your thoughts," and you find single pennies on your birthday or hers. Or if a favorite uncle always gave you commemorative quarters and when you occasionally find them, they're often for your uncle's home state. Sometimes the date stamped on the mysterious coin has significance, such as the date you were born or the date for others close to you, such as a child, were born. Coins that manifest at relevant times or in unusual places are a tangible "communication" that many of us would understand enough to reconsider their meaning beyond mere luck.

One of my favorite ways that loved ones in spirit can communicate is a similar manipulation: that of causing odors to fleetingly (or,

CHAPTER TWO

in some cases, lingeringly) waft around us. Our olfactory sense, meaning that of smell retention, is probably the strongest way we create an associative link in memory. For example, I was very close to my grandmother and whenever I think of her, I connect the scent of mothballs with memories of her because she used mothballs in everything! That smell is very distinctive and there's nothing else like it. Do you associate certain, pleasant aromas with someone, such as a perfume or a cooking scent with a mother figure that's passed on? Or an alcohol, aftershave, or tobacco scent with a father figure who's passed? Perhaps it is another pleasing smell that you correspond in memory with a loved one who is no longer in physical form.

Just like impressing a creature to appear and trigger a happy memory, our loved ones can cause the scent by which you would best remember them to temporarily fill the space around you. It may coincide with your thinking of them, or it may align with a special event, such as a family gathering, holiday, birthday, or anniversary. In my work as a psychic, I find this is a common means of communication that I then convey to my clients (because they're not smelling what I am). Sometimes a father figure will lovingly tease by making me smell the overwhelming scent of a cheap cologne that he received as a gift and obligingly doused himself with even though it wasn't his preference!

Another method by which our loved ones in spirit may make their presence known is through the manipulation of electricity. It is important to note that this should not be disruptive or frightening such as the lights in your room suddenly blowing. This will be another type of memory association by which programming on the television or radio will adjust to prompt an immediate association with a loved one, such as when you're driving along thinking about your favorite deceased aunt and in that precise moment her favorite song comes over the airwaves. Or the TV suddenly jumps channels to play an episode of a show in which a mother and daughter are making amends in the moment you are regretting that you and your mom left a lot of things unsaid. Occasionally, an electric light will gently flicker, such as the time my grandmother and I were looking at old pictures and remembering my grandfather; the lamp directly over us sputtered in the moment of highest emotional expression. In the room in which I do private readings, there's a night light that is always plugged in and turned on, but sometimes it flashes wildly as if to validate what I'm communicating to a client. It's comforting to interpret this as spiritual backup.

Once I received a phone call that was a wrong number, but I believe it may have been spiritually orchestrated to prepare me for bad news. One Sunday morning in January 2003, I was thinking of my dear friend Evelyn, an elderly woman who lived about two hours away. I found myself wondering how she was, when I'd hear from her next, and if she'd write or call. A while later that morning, the phone rang and a woman's voice asked for "Evelyn." When I told her she had dialed the number incorrectly, the woman said in a very warm, almost compassionate voice, "Oh, I'm so very sorry." At about 6:30 p.m. that evening, Evelyn's daughter called to tell me that Evelyn had passed away the previous Friday.

In very rare instances, a loved one who has passed on will actually leave a voice message on an answering machine or other recording device. I have had this reported to me a number of times over the years from clients who have tape recorded their psychic readings with me, although this is generally quite uncommon. In one example, a client asked a question to which I replied that it wasn't important for her to know the answer just yet. On the playback, a voice immediately preceding mine allegedly said, "Don't tell her that." In another instance I was sharing the green-glass turtle story, telling how no one knew how it got on the cemetery headstone or who put it there, and allegedly there was soft voice that answered, "Mikalah." Another time, I was assuring someone about something connected to an oversight or mistake of her father's that was followed by a male voice that said, "I didn't know." Now, I'm a highly skeptical person and I have very high standards for myself. I will disclose that I have never heard any of the preceding recordings, so I cannot vouch for their authenticity; sometimes people hear what they want to hear.

But once I did receive a CD in the mail from a client who had recorded her psychic reading with me. The voices on it are truly extraordinary. At one point in her psychic reading, I informed my client that I foresaw the potential for her to have another child if she so desired one. She responded by indicating that having another baby was not likely as she was in her early forties and she already had a twenty-one year old and a seven year old. But I reminded her that having another child could "look" a lot of different ways, such as foster or adoptive parenting, babysitting, or child care. Then I said, "I'm seeing a little boy." While my client thought it was intriguing, she wasn't quite convinced and we moved on. But in that moment on the recording playback, I swear, there's a *child's voice* that clearly says, "I'm ready for you." (She later told me that when she got home and broached the subject of another child with her husband, he said he had been thinking about it but just hadn't told her yet.) As her psychic reading concluded, my client was saying goodbye to me while rifling through her purse for her car keys. Her recorder was still running during this time though she could not find her keys. At one point she dumped out the contents of her purse to no avail. After about ten minutes, she finally found her car keys *in her purse*! On the recording playback, there's a woman's voice—a very ordinary-sounding voice, actually—that interjects with, "Please stop her." In debriefing, we both interpreted this as a moment of divine intervention in which a loved one in spirit, or maybe even an angel, had deliberately detained my client for her own safety (who knows, if she had left on time she might've been in an accident).

Instead of a recording, sometimes people will audibly hear the voice of a loved one that has passed on, perhaps reassuring them or cautioning them. Also less common is when a small object that we associate in memory with a loved one reappears out of place, such as finding your great-grandfather's old pocket watch in the middle of your bed instead of locked away in your jewelry box, where it's always been for safekeeping. Examples similar to these should not be frightening experiences but, instead, should be sentimental reminders that we are still connected to our loved ones despite their transition from the physical world to the Heavenly realm.

On occasion, the soul energy of a loved one in spirit will make its presence known in photographs or videos, usually in the form of an airborne sphere called an *orb*. In my experience, I have found that orbs representing the soul energy of someone who has passed on will manifest at times of high, loving, and positive emotion. This typically occurs at reunions, birthdays, and anniversaries, holidays, or the birth of a new baby—times when family members are gathered together and, perhaps, sharing memories that include the dearly departed. In one instance, the patriarch of a family "took" his place in a family portrait by appearing as a white orb in an appropriate and unobtrusive position—precisely where one might expect him to stand. In another picture, two teenage brothers pose next to the grave marker of a baby brother who had died in infancy. Right beside them is a perfectly-formed round orb. In a couple examples, I have consecutive photographs in which orbs appear, taken seconds apart. In both situations, the orbs have *moved* location and intensified in size or appearance. In both instances, there was a loving bond between the individuals in the pictures, such as the mother and daughter who joined hands together as an orb blossomed into an effervescent *swoosh* in front of them. Orbs can be white or a golden hue or sometimes soft blue, violet, or rose-colors. I have also seen videos of orbs seemingly materializing out of nowhere and quickly traveling and bobbing about.

I was once explaining orbs to a young man who was recently married. He said there was a rather pronounced orb in one of his wedding pictures. When we took a look, there it was: imprinted directly over top of where his hand clasped that of his new bride's for their first dance. His wife believed it was the essence of her stepfather, with whom she had been quite close. I knew that on occasion, if you enlarged orb photos electronically, you could see interesting or unusual shapes and patterns. Fortunately, my friend had the same picture on his computer and we blew it up for a close-up view of the orb. I've never seen anything like it before or since! It looked exactly like a rose in bloom, with perfectly-scalloped edges and rows of petals within petals. It was truly a gift from Heaven, in my opinion and in that of my friends.

UNDER SPIRITUAL SIEGE

GHOSTS I'VE KNOWN

Our soul energy is the invisible equivalent of musical DNA. That is, we are all assigned a note on the grand scale of the Universe that is uniquely our own. Our soul vibrates at this note in order to distinguish us from all others in the same manner that no two human beings are exactly alike. Such is the case for all those we have known and loved who have shed their physical bodies and exist in Heaven. Those souls are aware that we cannot see or hear how to identify their special "musical note," so in order to communicate with us they will generally use one or more of the methods explained in the preceding chapter.

Now, allow me to explain the difference between the spirit of a loved one who has passed on and a ghost. A spirit is a human soul that has left its physical body by virtue of the dying process and successfully transitioned—or crossed over or passed on—to the Heavenly realm. You may have seen mediums, such as John Edward, feel as though they are perceiving the presence of a family relative, but will ask the family members if the individual in question is living or passed. This isn't a means of bluffing; the question gets asked because our loved ones in spirit don't make the distinction between a finality that we have defined as "life" and "death." To them, it is *all* a form of life, just in different forms.

When making their presence known on the Earth plane, spirits will retain aspects of their personality that will make them readily identifiable to their loved ones, including their sense of humor. Most significant to know, however, is this important rule of thumb: *a loving presence will only ever be a loving presence.* So while a loving presence may incorporate cuss words to jokingly demonstrate the playful side of their personality, a loving presence would never swear with anger in an abusive or disrespectful manner.

On the other hand, a ghost, or discarnate spirit, is a human soul that has left its physical body as a result of the dying process but has *not* transitioned and has, instead, remained earthbound. (Some people refer to ghosts as *spirits* and that is their prerogative, but I will distinguish a ghost by calling it such.) This can occur due to a sudden death, which may leave the soul dazed and confused, such as a car accident. If you look up the aftermath of the September 11, 2001, United Flight 93 plane crash in Shanksville, Pennsylvania, you will learn that for several months afterward, security guards assigned to protect the site saw and heard very unusual activity, including voices and footsteps. Some of the guards saw what looked like real people and actually identified these individuals as crash victims by looking at photographs of those who had perished.

A ghost may also refuse to transition to the Heavenly realm due to strong negative human emotions they were experiencing at the time of their death, such as rage, revenge, jealousy, depression, and so on—these are emotions not found in the Heavenly realm. Others may lag behind temporarily, not fully realizing they are dead. Some ghosts are the souls of people who were raised to believe in a vengeful, wrathful God who will punish them by banishing them to hell. They are so afraid that it is easier to cling to an earthbound existence even if it's only half existing.

On a side note, when is a ghost not a ghost? When it's a "spontaneous replay." For example, the Gettysburg battlefield has long been the subject of paranormal intrigue. It was the physical site of extremely high, dramatic human emotion. There were tens of thousands of violent casualties—young men who were slaughtered in battle, who were seriously wounded, and those who later succumbed to their injuries. There is a lot of quartz in the Gettysburg area; some of the original homesteads were built on quartz. It is thought that, under the proper atmospheric conditions, the intense energy of a specific incident, retained in the quartz, is "released" and replays in the form of a ghostly tableau, like soldiers not thought to be Civil War reenactors suddenly appearing on the battlefield. In such documented circumstances, it is not a case of

UNDER SPIRITUAL SIEGE

human souls "trapped" or earthbound but is, instead, a case of a rare phenomenon replaying a fragment of history captured in time and emotionally embedded in the environment.

Thus when the tragedy is especially violent, such as a brutal murder or a mass killing, the emotion linked to the incident creates an impression on the immediate environment. Think of it like leaving your fingerprints behind after having been in someone's bathroom. What remains is nearly invisible information about your presence long after the fact. One way to interpret the ghosts witnessed in tragic environments is to reconcile that their souls have crossed over, but their emotional "fingerprints" are left behind. Theoretically, under the proper conditions those fingerprints become visible momentarily. What triggers the instant replay may be a combination of atmospheric conditions, such as mist or fog, or emotional conditions, such as someone mourning or thinking about the lives lost in the environment. It's fascinating to speculate that bits of history past are embedded in certain environments, frozen in time and awaiting the next time the spiritual play button gets pressed.

Beware anyone who may seem to exaggerate or sensationalize the subject matter to heighten the fear factor or deliberately create an aura of eeriness. This can reflect an unhealthy stereotype. Instead, I would like to make a plea on behalf of all ghosts for our consideration.

In my work as a psychic, I encounter both spirits and ghosts. Because of their high-vibration, upper-tier locale, spirits are light and loving and focused on communicating positive messages to their family and friends who are missing them. Remember, in Heaven there are no low-vibration, negative emotions such as greed or selfishness. While a spirit retains aspects of its human personality, they now enjoy 360-degree vision, such that they are aware of their faults and shortcomings when in human form, and will often accept responsibility for such. Ghosts are different because they are one step removed from functioning in what we perceive as our dimensional reality. Unlike spirits, they have not transitioned, so ghosts can still retain disturbing and distressing human emotions. As noted, sometimes a human soul will not transition immediately due to a very sudden, unexpected, or tragic passing that causes temporary confusion or disorientation. This generally passes within anywhere from a few days to a few weeks at most, and in my psychic work I have "seen" an angel or grandparent come to retrieve them if they do not eventually figure it out on their own. But in my experience, I tend to attract another breed of ghosts.

Maybe it's because I've worked on the periphery of the mental health field since 1987, but I often channel the ghosts of angry young men who were addicts, alcoholics, abusers, murderers or who were murdered, or who overdosed, committed suicide, etc.—and I allow them to come through. I grant permission to channel them despite their bitterness or rage, and despite the foul language that I am compelled to use because it feels like a sneeze that just *has* to come out (and amid my embarrassment, their family and friends always confirm, "That's exactly how he talked!").

I receive these angry young men because I care. I allow for them to come through because I have tremendous compassion for them. And I treat them with respect and sensitivity. We ordinarily honor the departed with reverence and respect, but why not those who are departed and stuck? Instead, some will chastise and provoke them, further exacerbating their circumstances, increasing their negative energy, and contributing to their overall confusion. But we must remember: we're talking about human souls who struggled in human form and are still continuing to struggle. They require a kinder, gentler approach. This does not mean befriending or enabling them but assuming the role of a firm teacher to enlighten them and illuminate the truth of their circumstances. Hopefully, this position will set a new standard and create an enhanced awareness for all those who only know of ghosts in the traditional moaning, wailing, and chain-rattling stereotype.

I actually got the opportunity to experience what it's like to "be" a ghost, and maybe that has also enhanced my empathy for them. It occurred in the context of a vivid dream, so vivid that I almost wondered if I was glimpsing a snippet of a previous lifetime. In the dream I was a gangster who belonged to a 1940s-era Chicago mob, and who was gunned down in a police raid. I remember the sensation of bullets hitting my body like slugs pummeling dead meat. But I also remember feeling as though nothing was wrong with me, thinking to myself, "Ha! They didn't get me!" Of course no one could've survived the kind of violent assassination I endured, but it didn't feel that way to me. In fact, I still felt the same as I had before, only things were somehow "off" around me. Everything seemed a bit hazy or gray like in a dream, and I could go where I wanted to just by thinking about it (lacking a physical body). I lost all track of time as well. I decided to take revenge by infiltrating a police barracks during a meeting. I threw papers into the air and collapsed bleachers, causing fear and disruption. I felt invisible and omnipotent . . . until I was seen by a child. Then I knew with certainty that I wasn't as invisible as I thought I was. I awakened with this new knowledge and new understanding of how it must feel to be earthbound and how, ultimately, it's a rather lonely, solitary existence.

CHAPTER THREE

One of my earliest direct encounters with a ghost—or what I thought was a ghost—also occurred in a dreamlike state when I was a boy. I was napping during the afternoon at a time when I was depressed, and I dreamt that something physically struck me. The dream was vivid, and in it, I was knocked to the floor by a dark force. I looked up to see it, gray and misty, swirling above me in a human-looking shape. In that moment, I awoke to discover myself on the floor having fallen out of bed, which never happened before or since.

In 2002, I had a close encounter with a ghost in which I actually made physical contact with it! It was over the Christmas holiday and I was visiting some family friends out of state. The first evening I stayed with them, we watched their two-and-a-half-year-old daughter spontaneously interact with her "imaginary friend" Elliott (named after the protagonist in *E.T. the Extra-Terrestrial*, her favorite movie). It was the oddest thing. Right in the middle of playing, she dropped what she was doing, ran to a corner of the room, and started talking into thin air, nodding her head and answering questions out loud in what was a two-way conversation. For example, she would jabber something, pause and then reply, "My pajamas." That night I prayed that the presence was pure, but I wasn't so sure.

On Christmas morning just after 3:00 a.m., I got up to go to the bathroom, located just outside the bedroom in which I was staying. As I returned to the bedroom, I closed the door with my right hand, and turning my body, the fingertips of my left hand brush against *something*. It felt just as if I had touched a person. Startled, I gasped out loud, and, looking, waved my hand in the air to see how it was possible. But there was nothing. The only thing I could've brushed was the edge of a hardwood dresser, and that wasn't it. The first thing I thought of was "Elliott." Feeling unnerved, I got back into bed, and prayed that the presence would do no harm, especially to my friend's little girl. But this was the same bedroom where, two years prior, a pair of navy blue socks disappeared from my suitcase and reappeared the next morning, unused—I was sleeping on one, and the other was on the floor next to the bed. Clearly there was something odd going on in this house.

That evening, I had a private conversation with the mother of the little girl about her talking to Elliott. I shared my experience from early that morning. The mother reminded me that on one of my first days there, I said I'd heard a cat mew, which I did (the noise came from inside the house, but this family had no cats). She said that, for reasons unknown, they have always associated cats with her daughter, and even call her "alley cat." She also said that when the girl was an infant, she slept in the same room I was staying in, and one day her grandmother heard the baby "talking" two hours after being put down for a nap. When the grandmother picked her up, the girl turned toward the window and was still talking to "someone." The mother said that the conversations with Elliott began the spring prior, at the time of great marital discord.

I had gently cautioned this family about the presence and its side effects. But not everyone is open to hearing such unconventional perspectives and I had to tread very carefully seeing as how they were family friends. Ultimately, there was no follow up and the deterioration persisted within the household and, particularly, within the family unit. The little girl developed anger management issues for which she required therapy, her older sister became anorexic and was frequently hospitalized, and the marriage ended in a bitter divorce. It was an invaluable lesson in the kind of negative influence parasitic energies, like ghosts, can have over others, especially those who are oblivious to the obvious in terms of what is transpiring around them in plain view.

Ghosts are not unreachable, however. Oftentimes, they welcome the chance to be heard and to present their side of things. Remember, they are formerly human beings clinging to human sentiments that are holding them down. There have been times for which I was asked to assess a "haunted" environment in advance of a speaking engagement and the presences actually reached out to connect with me in dreams *in advance*.

On one occasion, I was to conduct a psychic gallery at an Italian restaurant that had been a church for decades with a room for funeral viewings in the basement. Prior to entering into a situation like this, I want to know absolutely nothing about anything. But in the days prior to my initial visit, I had a couple of odd dreams. "They" showed me that, in the basement, there was a secret room or special compartment with a dirt floor. I was also shown how they had exerted their presence over some of the employees. One in particular, who was finishing up some work alone late one night, vowed he wasn't returning after he was spooked. Most fascinating was the dream in which about two or three of "them" (males) showed me how they levitate metal objects. They used a visual analogy to explain that it was mentally the same as lighting fire to a piece of paper; it takes a moment for the paper to ignite and curl before it gains momentum and goes up in flame. So when I got to the restaurant, I already knew to ask about the secret room (sure enough, there it was with a dirt floor and walls), disembodied men's voices (true, and they sounded harsh), and the rattling about of pots and pans (true again). After this initial investigation, I returned a second time to assist the owner to spiritually clear the space and send the presences Heavenward.

I find that most often, ghosts are males. This makes sense to me in that males tend not to be as sensitive or intuitive as females. They also tend to be disbelievers—sometimes stubbornly so—in most things that are without logical explanation. Therefore, male ghosts are generally very angry, aggressive, and bitter, afraid to release themselves and gravitate to the Heavenly realm for fear of being rejected and sent to hell. Also, there is no such thing as "ghost rehab," and so the mental-emotional wellness issues and addictions that plagued them in human form still persist. Sometimes, this translates into very violent behavior such as pushing, kicking, pinching, or scratching. Objects may be knocked over, thrown, or broken. Angry voices that curse and growl may be heard. On rare occasion, a young woman may feel as though she's being stalked in her own home, usually in the bathroom and bedroom where she is nude and most vulnerable. As such, ghosts usually exist in association with specific environments.

Female ghosts tend to be benign. Usually, they are victims of homicide, have perished in an accident, or were depressed and suicidal prior to their passing. Sometimes, if they were dominated by a male in real life, I see that they remain under such control in ghost form. On one occasion, I was scheduled for a live, in-person radio interview at a small, rural station that had been experiencing some paranormal activity that included doors opening and closing and knocking noises. As with the restaurant, I had dreams prior to actually being on site. In the dreams, which occurred over two consecutive nights, I was a female passenger in a car that flipped over and started filling up with water. My sense was that her dying thoughts were of care and concern for her children. I saw her running to the radio station to inform them. Equipped with this information, I knew to share the dreams with my hosts at the radio station.

Amazingly, one of them told me an incident identical to what I described had happened to a family member not far from the station. His family member was male, likely the driver, but there was a female in the car. Both drowned; but I stated that I felt it was the female who was trying to communicate her worries over her children. I rationalized that if she died under tragic or questionable circumstances (alcohol may have been involved or it may have been an abusive relationship), and the radio station was nearby, wouldn't it make sense to want to tell the very people who report the news? When I physically walked through the building, I mentally gave her permission to release while offering assurances that her children were okay. When I checked six months later, all disruptive activity had ceased.

This incident is similar, though slightly different, from another in which I believe the deceased mother in question was not a ghost but a spirit that had delayed her transition. The incident took place late Friday evening, March 6, 2015. Twenty-five-year-old Lynn Groesbeck's red Dodge sedan hit a cement barrier on a bridge and flipped upside down in the Spanish Fork River about fifty miles south of Salt Lake City, Utah. Groesbeck appeared to have perished on impact, but her eighteen-month-old daughter Lily was with her, strapped in a car seat in the back seat. Lily was suspended upside down, with ice-cold water rushing through broken windows just inches from her head. Groesbeck's vehicle was not visible from the road, so there Lily remained without food or water and in freezing overnight temperatures for an incredible fourteen hours until she was rescued.

The partially submerged vehicle wasn't discovered until about 12:30 p.m. on Saturday, March 7. Three police officers and two firemen who arrived on the scene all experienced something truly extraordinary when they happened upon the overturned vehicle: all of them heard an adult voice calling for help that was emanating from *inside the car*. The voice was so clear and distinct that the first responders replied to it, calling out to hang in there. The voice couldn't have been that of Groesbeck, already deceased; nor could it have come from baby Lily. Fork City police officer Jared Warner said the voice calling for help was as plain as day and did not sound like a child.

If one eyewitness attested to hearing a mysterious voice pleading for rescue, it might be explained by the adrenaline of high emotion or a trick of natural acoustics. But in this instance, a team of five trained professionals all reported hearing the same voice, which led to the miraculous recovery of baby Lily. I believe that Lynn Groesbeck's spirit remained with Lily in that overturned vehicle through the long, cold night and into the following afternoon, fueled by something that even her death could not sever: a mother's love for her baby. Any way you choose to look at it, Lily's rescue is an amazing story of divine intervention.

While female ghosts tend to be more passive than males, the male ghosts are not beyond redemption, it just takes longer to wear them down. But one of the wonderful things about being human is that we are programmed to respond to kindness.

On the evening of June 13, 2013, I began a psychic gallery session of about thirty people. After an opening prayer, I immediately felt a male presence move in. This presence made me feel as though I had been hit multiple times in the gut. I was also smelling alcohol. Brandi, a young woman in the audience, raised her hand and said that her cousin, Travis, had been shot to death with multiple hits to the stomach. Travis kept making me feel the hits to his gut, but he never acknowledged the gunshot to the head, which is what killed him. He had been alcoholic and was murdered at a halfway house in a dispute over a bottle of vodka. Travis died at age thirty-one on December 15, 2011, so he had been deceased for a year and a half at the time.

Travis quickly commandeered the session, telling Brandi—through me—that he thought of her as a sister (they were close in age and grew up together) and asking about the little girl he left behind, his eight-year-old daughter. He said he kept setting off a toy in her room, which Brandi confirmed but said the daughter was frightened when this happened. At one point, filled with paternal compassion, I assured Travis by saying, "It's all right, sweetheart," to which I heard Travis angrily retort, "I ain't no f**king f*gg*t!" In that exact moment I realized I was not dealing with a spirit who had crossed over to the Heavenly realm; I was dealing with a ghost. At that point, I quickly took back control and mentally told Travis to go stand in the corner until I was ready to deal with him further, which he did, sulking like a scolded child.

Before leaving that evening, I joined hands with Brandi to say a prayer for Travis. But on the ride home, I suddenly realized he was there with me, sitting in the passenger seat! I immediately said, "Oh no, this is *not* going to happen! I am not your ticket to feeling whole and human again," and with that, I mentally kicked him out.

On July 20, 2013, I had a day of psychic readings scheduled. My first client was Brenda, who looked familiar to me. She explained that she had been at the previous month's gallery, seated in front of Brandi, whom she knew peripherally. Brenda had brought a tape recorder to document her session. As soon as my prayer with Brenda was completed, I felt Travis move in. I told Brenda he was here and asked her what she wanted to do about it. She said she wanted her session and, if there was time left over, she would allow him to have his say. So I told Travis he needed to leave. He reacted by standing in the doorway to my room. But I told him he needed to leave the building. I next saw him standing outside on the stairs. I told him no, he must vacate the premises, and I heard him calling to me from the furthest edge of the parking lot. It was almost like sending a child to their room as punishment and having them continuously calling down the stairs, "Can I come out yet?"

Almost a year later, Brenda wrote me a letter explaining that her recording had lots of interruptions on it, some of which frightened her. At the onset of the recording, during my prayer with Brenda, there was a "roar." Interspersed was some inappropriate laughter and, in one spot, Travis saying, "I will f**k you up!" When Travis complained, through me, about holes in his stomach, Brenda heard gunshots on the tape. She said it was all so evil and hateful sounding that she got rid of it. My last client of the same day as Brenda's appointment also looked familiar to me when she came in. She reminded me that she was Brandi, Travis' cousin who had attended the psychic gallery in June. "But," she said, "the appointment's not for me. Here's Travis' mother, Sheri." I was so surprised! Travis and his mother had different last names, so when I saw my last client's name in my appointment book, a family connection never occurred to me. "Oh, my gosh," I exclaimed, "Travis was here this morning and I kicked him out!"

I knew that Sheri had come in with the hope of contacting Travis specifically, but I told her I couldn't make that guarantee. We sat down together, and Brandi joined us to offer Sheri her comfort and support. I said a prayer with Sheri and the first thing out of my mouth was, "Oh f**k, my mom's here!" What Sheri told me was that prior to his death, she and Travis had an argument and things were strained between them. What transpired over the next hour was something of a tug of war with Travis communicating things as pedestrian as "I miss eating hamburger and steak" (the family had just had a big cookout) to "I can't even take a f**king p*ss."

I saw an opportunity with these statements. You see, in order to help Travis transition, he had to come to the realization that a transition was necessary on his own. So I began the tedious process of wearing him down by asking leading questions such as, "Why can't you have a steak?" and "Why can't you urinate, Travis?" By the end of the hour he finally asked me, softly, "Am I a ghost?" With tears brimming in my eyes, I replied, "Yes, honey. You're a ghost." I instructed Travis to lift up his head and look for the pinpoint of light. If he moved toward it, it would grow bigger and brighter and Jesus would be there to welcome him. I assured him that he would not be turned away and that his daughter would be just fine. In fact, I said, his ability to connect with her would be magnified.

At the conclusion of her psychic reading, Sheri asked me if I would come to her home and bless the space, but I suggested we wait a week to see what Travis decides to do.

UNDER SPIRITUAL SIEGE

The very next day, I went for my usual afternoon walk. There's a portion of the trail that cuts through a wooded area and it is here that I always say the Lord's Prayer. Immediately after I concluded my prayer, there was Travis! But it wasn't the angry, sullen Travis I had come to know in a love-hate relationship. He showed himself as a ball of light, bouncing and cart-wheeling all over the place! He was hugging me and shaking my hand and saying uncharacteristic things like, "It's everything you promised it would be and more!" "Tell my mom that God is love," "Tell my family they need to forgive the other person," and "Tell my mom she has to help other moms going through the same thing." He next told me he always wanted to be a rock star, and, picking up a guitar, he began to play me the song "Free" by the group Phish. It was a tune he knew I'd recognize but its lyrics are also telling, talking about being free, feeling the sensation of weightlessness, and recalling dormant feelings. It was a communication in musical format that perfectly summarized his newfound release. Finally, Travis indicated that he was presented with a tantalizing incentive: his soul energy would be given the option of returning in human form as his daughter's first-born child in order to be close to her once again and to make amends for any time lost.

Because I had just said a prayer, I felt reasonably assured that it really was Travis I had encountered, but I was cautious about the extent to which my own imagination may have been at play. I decided to wait until the following day before contacting Travis' family. When I called Brandi, I said I thought I had some good news to share and arranged for the family to come to Alta View the next day to debrief.

The following evening, the entire family came in, about a dozen people, including Travis' father, brother, and Travis' young daughter (whom I asked to remain outside our meeting room with an aunt as I didn't wish to upset one so young). I began the meeting by reviewing the events of the past forty-eight hours, and how it was my opinion that Travis had successfully transitioned. Travis's mother Sheri had played the tape recording of her psychic reading for her husband; apparently during it, my voice changes, and Travis's father told me, "I heard my son's voice on that tape."

Sheri next shared that she also had a visit from Travis just hours before I did. She said she was lying in bed, thinking of Travis when her cell phone went off. It was a call from Travis's old cell phone—*which was in the room on her bureau top with his cremains*! When Sheri answered her phone, she heard only static. When she persisted in asking "Hello?" the static got louder and angrier-sounding, she said. Abruptly, the call shorted out. Our mutual interpretation was that it was Travis attempting to make one last go of it in his ghostly state before heeding my advice and giving a try at transitioning. I am proud to say that he succeeded!

As the meeting adjourned, Travis's father pulled me aside to say that for the first time in many months, Sheri was getting out of bed. She had been so devastated by Travis's murder that she slipped into a deep depression. But now she was rejuvenated and she was, indeed, counseling another mother who had lost a daughter tragically, just as Travis had requested.

I periodically encountered Travis in my meditations. As he hadn't finished school, he was also beaming with pride at the diplomas and certificates he showed me to indicate he was learning and graduating in his spiritual lessons. Once, he was dressed in a white cap and gown. He also expressed nothing but love and admiration for me anytime I would tell his story. But he would always be there to chime in with the request that I qualify the unpleasantness by informing all, "That was the *old* Travis."

Six months after Travis first appeared to me, I was scanning the online edition of my local newspaper and got a terrible, shocking surprise: there pictured at the top of the obituaries was Sheri! She had died at age forty-nine on January 16, 2014. Apparently she was driving Travis's daughter and a friend to school that morning and hit a patch of black ice. Sheri was thrown from the vehicle, but both little girls were unharmed. It was a bittersweet irony and I was so grateful to have facilitated a valuable healing for Sheri in the time that I knew her.

I still see Travis from time to time. He showed me that he was signed up for an internship by which he was like the Walmart greeter for other souls like him who were crossing over. He and Sheri reunited, but they are not existing in the same immediate space with one another; Travis continues his spiritual schooling in a separate area.

I went for an afternoon walk on July 25, 2014, little more than a year after I had first aided Travis to make an authentic choice about his existence. At one point, I began to think of him and wondered if he had advanced far enough along to know how to send a message or create a sign in the manner that I've outlined that those in spirit may do most commonly. But I dismissed it and walked on. About a block beyond, I turned and saw a beautiful fawn standing there, staring at me. It wasn't afraid nor did it retreat. I smiled to myself, knowing that Travis would always be my good buddy and special helper.

UNDER SPIRITUAL SIEGE

Chapter Four

DEMONS I'VE ENCOUNTERED

Demons comprise an intensely evil energy with an agenda of chaos and destruction. They are purportedly fallen angels that have rejected God. They refuse to acknowledge that they originated from the same glorious and good source that we all did. Demons have not been human so they are without the human agenda of ghosts, who tend to be immersed in their own unresolved issues. Ghosts will create disturbances because they feel their space is being disrupted or intruded upon, and they want the intruders to vacate and leave them alone. Demons, however, actively roam the universe preying upon the weak, such as children and those with addictions, and influencing the powerful, such as those who profit from manipulating others. Their ultimate goal is to instigate a momentum that culminates in a murder-suicide situation. They may achieve their goal through several routes.

Demonic malevolence is often duplicitous, meaning demons will masquerade as something they are not in order to gain someone's trust. For example, they may physically appear to manifest as a loved one who has passed, appearing in real time or in dreams, but only as a mimic; the demons cannot authentically replicate the presence of a loved one's spirit and so something will always be "off," such as the eye color or tone of voice. In February 2015, Melbourne, Australia, Bishop Peter Elliott told *The Sydney Morning Herald*:

> I know of a case of a woman who claimed she had an angel guiding her and she used to talk to this angel . . . but it finally showed its true face and revealed it was a liar. It wanted control, power over her. She was on the way to [demonic] possession; I'd say she was halfway there. But she got spiritual help and is now happy.

Demons will also target children and teenagers who are innocent or vulnerable, such as the teen who is perceived as a social outcast, by communicating that they are a friend. The demon will say things such as "I'm the only one who really cares," or "I'm the only true friend you've got." They do this subliminally by whispering from the background of the music or video games played by the child or teenager. In other instances, they will flat-out terrorize people in order to exacerbate tension within the household, one's school, or community. For example, in May 2014, two Waukesha, Wisconsin, schoolgirls repeatedly stabbed a classmate to appease "Slender Man," a tall, thin, featureless phantom. One of the girls was found to have drawn this character at least sixty times and mutilated Barbie dolls with his "symbol." Other recorded accounts similarly link violence against others with Slender Man. While Slender Man is a fictional creation dating to 2009, the negativity its association perpetuates is very real and destructive.

Another theory that is perhaps these entities don't originate from outside ourselves. If we all have "higher selves"—an ultimate version of our individual potential—could the manifestation of harmful, negative energies represent our "lower selves"? Could they be a grotesque reflection of our worst potential for harm and destruction? It's fascinating to ponder this internal power struggle.

I've also seen how such negative energy transfers from person to person if one is unprotected spiritually or otherwise unaware. A client of mine recently had an *aha! moment* for realizing why, as a hairdresser, she felt drained after shampooing and cutting certain individuals' hair. In my psychic work I have seen this happen particularly to people who do hands-on work with those who have physical ailments, especially anyone who works in the medical community, or as a massage therapist or chiropractor. If they do not protect themselves properly in prayer before touching others, these practitioners run the risk of assimilating some of the negative energy, depending upon the fitness of their own mental, physical, and spiritual well-being. Or they risk transferring it to others in their household for—literally—bringing their work home with them. Once I was giving a psychic reading to a young woman who had this very issue unbeknownst to her. Whenever I see negative energy attached to someone, it shows itself in the form of giant, three-foot-long black leeches hanging off the person, sucking them dry of any positive energy. This is what I saw for her and I gently told her so, which puzzled her although she did say that she was seeing human-shaped shadows in her apartment. I also felt that she was surrounded by unhealthy people with addictions. It was a classic case of psychic amnesia because she finally realized what I had told her was true. She was working as a bartender and was, of course, constantly around people with alcohol dependency issues. She was bringing home negative energy that had attached to her. I have also seen this in mental health and substance abuse counselors who are in regular contact with people struggling with their emotional well-being or addictions.

Pornography is another way in which demonic energy infiltrates and manipulates others, particularly men. Its accessibility is just a mouse click away. Porn has become increasingly graphic and violent. Its portrayal of insensitivity is commonplace. There is a trend toward porn renditions of Disney and other popular cartoon characters, which sullies what was originally intended to be pure and childlike. A sampling of porn company names is also reflective of the dark side: Diabolic, Black Market Video, Evil Angel, Treasure Island Media (its emblem is a skull with crossed swords), Devil's Film, Kink.com (which incorporates a devil's tail in its logo), Digital Sin, Sinner's Club, and Burning Angel. People will advocate the right to view whatever they want and that porn is harmless but it has become completely mainstream; its performers have become celebrities or have influenced others to emulate them in popular culture. (And where many current celebrities are concerned, irresponsible behavior is condoned and encouraged. There are celebrities who count among their status symbols their criminal convictions.)

Further, the line between pornography and how violence is depicted in popular entertainment has been blurred. In the past decade, a new genre of horror movie has emerged in which victims are graphically tortured in gratuitous and prolonged acts of sadism. There's even a term for it: "torture porn."

By encountering negative energies and comprehending how they work through human beings, I have to know what I'm up against. I refuse to watch torture porn films in their entirety, but I have watched select scenes from them on YouTube. Viewing these very brutal clips has an immediate effect on me. I physically tremble and my mood is affected; I become "dense," irritable, and depressed—which is precisely the intended outcome. Even as I write this, I feel myself becoming "down" and agitated simply from recalling those experiences. I can see how repeatedly watching pornography that degrades and dehumanizes others, and viewing horror films and video games that are "heavy" with hopelessness and inhumane acts will desensitize those affected over time. Not only that, like any harmful substance, once the initial thrill of the high wears off, the user is propelled to seek a more intense high, and a downward spiral initiates in which selfishness prevails, relationships are destroyed, and deception reigns.

Of course, manipulating individuals vulnerable to addiction is a classic form of demonic coercion, and John understands the destructive spiral that drug and alcohol dependency can engender. For a number of years of his life, he was selfish with a temper that was quick to flare, because getting angry became increasingly easier. He also found that he attracted like-minded individuals, such that anything positive was pushed aside. At social gatherings, John would find himself gravitating toward the "partyer" or the person getting high. During this period, he avoided looking in the mirror. It was disconcerting because when he did, he saw the reflection of his face mysteriously shift and divide. After numerous incarcerations, John had an epiphany while in prison. He began to read the Bible daily, and reclaimed his relationship with God. When John asked God for His help and His will, John said it was like the weight of the world was removed. After this, his healing and recovery began; but the same cannot be said for countless others who succumbed to their addictions.

It is in this manner that demonic energies operate in modern times. The old adage "you are what you eat" pertains not just to what you feed your body, but what you feed *your mind*. As with any potentially harmful material, it's not okay to suggest that because "other people do it," or because it's mainstream, it's all right for you. Such matters need to be evaluated on a person-by-person basis, based upon what amount, if any, is right for *you* as an individual. Even the slightest sip of alcohol can cause an alcoholic to rationalize themselves into a total relapse. So, if you take exception and desire to continue watching horror movies or playing violent video games, the choice is yours: you can either feed it or starve it.

Another instance of the manipulative, insidious pull of dark material is the current preoccupation with zombies, fictional, human corpses

UNDER SPIRITUAL SIEGE

that reanimate into cannibalistic beings devoid of human emotions. Zombies are no longer relegated to the occasional horror film but have, instead, gone mainstream, appearing in television commercials and programming, video games, and merchandise of all kind. The concept of zombies has made very dark material acceptable in popular culture, and reinforces a growing indifference or sense of competition toward others like ourselves for being "non-entities."

I had my own encounter with what I believe was a demonic presence when I was eleven. This was the period of the "dark man" which I referenced in chapter one. In hindsight it makes perfect sense that at this time I was an easy mark. I was depressed and socially ostracized. I spent most of my time alone, attracted to dark subject matter, as I mentioned. Coinciding with all of this was the appearance of the dark man in my bedroom doorway each night as I lay in bed. I could hear his approaching footsteps in my head and soon enough there he'd be: a black silhouette over six feet tall with a large broad-brimmed hat and a floor-length coat. He was there to consummate my desire to attain power over others, particularly my tormentors. Somehow I was wise enough to resist him, but every night I underwent the same routine, and every night I refused him. Eventually he stopped coming around. But as an adult, I came to understand that the dark man is actually a universally seen specter, who sometimes has red eyes. Decades later, I was talking with a coworker about negative energies and he told me about how his two young sons insisted that something kept staring in through their bedroom window at night. Without me saying a word, my friend described exactly what I had seen all those years ago. In fact, he said, his boys were so adamant that he scattered sawdust under their bedroom window to see if he could capture any footprint impressions (not surprisingly, he didn't).

Nowadays, I found that the presence I once knew as the "dark man" is called "Hat Man." Someone posted his personal encounter to an online message board devoted to such experiences:

I saw the "Hat Man" around the year 1990, when I was twenty-three. I had been messing around with a Ouija board and doing drugs with my girlfriend, at the time, at her house. Something must've followed me home, because I would wake up in the middle of the night and see these animal shadows running across my room for a couple months. I later learned that these shadow animals are like scouts that go before the main entity. Then one night I woke up and saw this large black shadow at the foot of my bed with a wide-brimmed hat, big coat, red glowing eyes, and a huge smile on his face with large pointy white teeth, reaching to strangle me. I totally freaked out and started kicking, yelling, and swinging at it and it disappeared immediately. I never saw it again. I looked on the Internet ten years later and couldn't believe how many people had seen the same thing. I believe it feeds off fear, or just wanted to scare the crap outta me. I also believe that using the Ouija board and doing drugs brought it into my life, as I am a Christian and this was a sad time for me in my life since I wasn't praying or reading the Bible at the time. I still think about it from time to time, only because of how many have seen the creature all over the world. I had some very strange things happen to both me and my girlfriend from using the Ouija board and would hope that anyone reading this will take it as a warning to stay very far away from them, as they only bring evil into your life.

What I found in my work as an autism consultant was that any number of children and teens on the autism spectrum also had similar things happening. Two mitigating factors corroborated these experiences. First, people with autism tend to be very literal and concrete in what they interpret around them; therefore, they tend not to lie and when they do it's usually transparent. Second, I collected anecdotes gleaned from my work in which people with autism from all over my home state and beyond were telling me the same things without ever having met one another. (This was also long before people began connecting in globally pervasive ways through social media.) What was most intriguing to me was that the kids and teens who identified demons in their lives all conveyed that each entity was a persona non grata (the literal Latin interpretation of which means "an unwelcome person"). That is, so entrenched are these presences in their servitude to the great deceiver that they are absent of their own identities. They have adopted ambiguous and indistinct monikers such as "No Name," "Mr. Nobody," "No One Who Came From Nowhere," "X," and "Any"—all reminiscent of the scene in *The Exorcist* in which a tape recording of a supposed demon's voice sounds like gibberish, but when it's played in reverse, it audibly reveals, "I am no one."

In one case, Brett, a twenty-year-old client was adamant that "his" demon, named "Zero," was not intentionally causing him harm. Zero was a presence that Brett could not hear or see but he definitely sensed. When interviewing Brett, I held firmly (but gently) to my beliefs that anything other than a loving presence was ill-intended and possessed its own agenda. He was defensive and bristled when I described such presences as "parasitic." When I listed the ways an ill-intended presence might manifest, I suggested sleep disturbance and there was a noticeable shift in Brett's facial expression, almost a smirk.

Brett said Zero is with him for life now, and is the opposite of him and that he is a good person. He also described kicking a demon out of his life that, as a result, is now missing an arm and a foot. It had approached him about recruiting Brett for, as he put it, Hell's Army. He said that Zero was afraid once and precluded him from entering a church wedding. Afterwards, Brett's caseworker explained that Brett's parents were divorcing. Zero apparently "woke up" from a dormant state about the time of all the tension and angst at home. Brett began talking about Zero tenfold, and has even "zoned" out in public because of Zero. Brett has no motivation to better himself through education or a job, although he denied being intruded upon or manipulated.

After my interview with Brett, his caseworker followed up with me again. Brett wanted me to know that Zero *does* have an agenda, but Brett does not feel that either Zero or Zero's agenda is all evil. Brett said, "His origin is demonic, but his personality is not." When she and Brett began to talk about God, Brett said he didn't always "buy into it totally," especially after Zero appeared. He started to really question God. Brett's caseworker countered by telling him that it sounded like Zero *was* starting his own agenda to pull Brett away from God and bring him over to a darker side. Brett was defensive, and said that Zero has nothing to do with his questioning his spirituality. Zero just happened to be "awakened" at the same time.

Similar to Brett, another client, a fifteen-year-old girl, confided that she had grappled with the presence of a "demon" (her word). She indicated that it temporarily subsided, but that, in recent times, it had returned. She does not perceive the demon as harming her and missed it previously because she was "lonely." Another client, a seventeen-year-old male, had been in psychiatric hospitalization three times in five months for seriously cutting himself and inserting objects into his penis. I learned that he grew up in an abusive alcoholic environment prior to residential placement. He was living with his grandparents most recently. He has reported hearing voices of men and seeing black shapes or shadows telling him to harm himself. He reports this immediately after he's harmed himself.

One could speculate that the preceding instances could be attributed to "attention-seeking behavior" or an overactive imagination, but when things start affecting other family members in the same household, there's reason to pause and assess what is truly going on. An eleven-year-old male client who had experienced sleep disturbances for years had recently begun having night terrors, complaining of monsters under his bed. He now takes Melatonin to help him sleep but will still awaken during the night (before 3:00 a.m.) and get into bed with his parents, even though he shares a bedroom with his brother. However, there had been some spill-over in real-time to validate the boy's fears.

The family dog had been overly anxious. One of the boy's brother's friends had seen and heard things in the house. The mother said she'd seen something move in the background in the mirror while drying her hair. Though she knew she was alone in the house, she'd still go and look for someone. And the boy's sister said that several times a bedroom lamp had changed location upon re-entering her bedroom. She also said she had heard "music-box music" outside her bedroom. Light bulbs have flickered or blown more than usual, the computer has malfunctioned, and small objects have gone missing and later turned up. In one instance, the boy's brother's iPod disappeared but reappeared in his school bag, which he had previously searched. Most disturbingly, the boy had become increasingly aggressive, usually toward his mother, who has been bitten by him. He's thrown knives out the window and crawled out onto the second floor roof with a knife. He has also screamed and cursed at Jesus Christ.

Employing my psychic intuition, I walked the house with them, feeling uncomfortable about the basement in particular. It felt very heavy. I had previously picked up a male and female presence, and felt the male in the basement, especially near a far corner. The father said that he works down in the basement and has felt uncomfortable, and the brother reported the boy had seen someone down there as well—someone with red, glowing eyes.

I next asked about the master bedroom, and there my stomach dropped, I got queasy, and my knees felt weak. I felt this space was the seat of a lot of stress and tension in the home, and the boy said he had seen the "man" seated on the bed in that room. Next was the attic where I felt a female presence. The boy's brother said his friend heard and saw a woman up there, too. Hearing voices is a commonly reported phenomena in haunting situations. But when an individual reports that they are hearing voices that others do not hear, they risk being diagnosed as schizophrenic or delusional with auditory hallucinations. Some people have been hearing voices all their lives, as I learned by visiting Intervoiceonline.org. While this group contends that people can learn to live with their voices and manage integrating them in their daily lives, others point to something more sinister.

On a public Intervoiceonline message board, one person wrote, "I need help, my boyfriend has voices in his head. . . He's been hearing the voice since about six years old after a lady killed herself right in front of him. . . . The voice made him try shooting someone in the leg (gun was empty), he killed animals. . . . Also, the voice told him to sell his soul to the devil." Another person said, "For the last five years I have been hearing cruel voices, mostly a man and a woman. They say sexually mocking stuff and put downs. They are cleverly monitoring everything I do, and are studied in all the subtleties of harassing a person into darkness and negativity. . . . I have come to believe they are part of the devil, and they found a way to get through to me psychicly." Someone else agreed, defining the voices as "so downright nasty and evil that they could not possibly be part of me. . . . The voices will do their utmost to use your past experiences to scare you, or make you uncomfortable about yourself."

Another person posting found a way to diminish the impact of the voices' deprecating comments by responding to them with, "Really? That may be so, but at least I know where my issues are and am working on them." Another strategy suggested was to simply ask the voices, "'What else do you suggest I do about it?' They will often respond with suggestions about things to do, usually harmful to yourself and others. Just ask, 'How will that help the situation?' Don't let them get away with making inappropriate comments. Keep saying, 'You haven't answered my question,' or repeating your question 'How will that be helpful?'"

There was a pervasive sense that the voices "do their best to deceive you. . . especially by creating a false sense of power and knowledge." But in general, the voices seemed possessed of ill intentions. "My voices aren't good or helpful," wrote another person grappling with this issue. "What I can make out from the whispering is about death, destruction, and torture." Someone else noted, "The voices in my head tell me to kill myself." A grown woman reported that she has heard them since she was a little girl. "Sometimes they haze me by telling me I'm stupid, or that I'm ugly, better off dead," she said. "Other times I hear other people suffering and crying . . ." Another person was definitive in stating that he feels the voices "are demons. I don't talk to them, but to God instead. Once you start talking to the voices, you elevate them to a position of authority to which they have no right." His antidote was "Treat yourself with love and respect and don't be too hard on yourself! Connect with your home and appreciate what you have. Try to 'pray the voices away'—remember they are demonic in most cases—and try to trust in God. Believe me, it's the only way and worth a try."

I have known people who struggled with drug addiction and reported hearing demonic voices urging them deeper into self-destruction. In other instances, people have acted upon the instruction of the voices to the point of committing murder. An exemplary case occurred in Naperville, Illinois, on Halloween eve, 2012. A forty-year-old woman was charged with first-degree murder in the slaying of her eight-year-old son and a five-year-old girl she was babysitting in a suburban Chicago townhouse. She had stabbed the children dozens of times—her son had more than 100 wounds. She had also stabbed to death two dogs in the house. She told police that she had heard "demonic voices" prior to the attack and felt the children had "evil inside them and she was trying to drive the devil out of them."

This example is becoming commonplace as attacks in our schools and communities become a nearly weekly occurrence. It calls into question the line between mental illness and demonic influence, and whether both experiences are really one in the same. A school psychologist who is a colleague of mine is becoming convinced of this theory. She reported to me the challenges of two students on her caseload. One, a ten-year-old female in third grade, is diagnosed with mood disorder not otherwise specified, psychotic disorder not otherwise specified and anxiety disorder. This little girl has described the malevolent "X-friend who comes from inside me." She repeatedly alleged that X-friend hurt her by hitting her and stabbing her with knives. The second student, a sixteen-year-old ninth grade boy, complained of seeing "black-cloaked figures" and "the gray man." The student was anxious and fearful of these figures, particularly the gray man, which sounded very much like my own dark man. His clinical diagnosis are major depressive disorder—recurrent with psychotic features.

Instead of supporting the individual—in these instances, children—to feel empowered to defend themselves, our culture's response has been to ascribe a mental illness diagnosis (or multiple diagnoses) and to treat the "hallucinations" with strong, anti-psychotic pharmaceuticals. But isn't this the same as taking Pepto-Bismol to contain one's nausea during a bout with the flu? The medicine may prevent you from vomiting, but you still have the flu! In other words, are we merely putting a Band-Aid over a much bigger issue: that of active spiritual warfare in which those who are innocent, weak, or vulnerable are being manipulated to harm themselves and others. In the spirit of knowledge is power, the next chapter examines symptoms of a haunting-type situation.

UNDER SPIRITUAL SIEGE

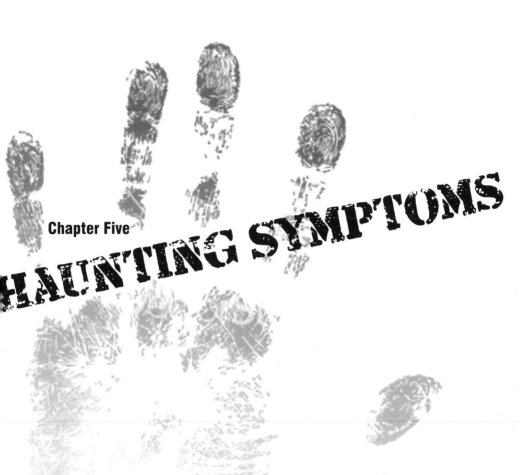

Chapter Five

HAUNTING SYMPTOMS

Many people have become conditioned by modern horror movies to believe that anything out of the ordinary is the manifestation of some kind of predatory evil. But not everything seemingly unusual is malicious, just misunderstood perhaps. It is important for family members and parents of children and teens to maintain a healthy skepticism as well as bear an open mind in investigating the information observed or shared by the individual. Remember: not everything is something, and some experiences may have logical explanations, such as the child who is verbally or physically replaying an authentic or fictional event. An example of this is the child who appears to be talking to someone unseen but is role-playing a favorite cartoon scene. In other instances, explanations for flickering lights could be attributed to faulty wiring. A small object moving on its own might've gained traction from the rattling vibrations of a train or a truck on the street outside. I've been witness to this myself when wine glasses in my china cabinet appear to have moved out of line from others; I know this is due to vibrations from my walking past the cabinet.

As has been previously discussed, there are ways in which a loving presence in spirit can communicate with us. Oftentimes children are the most susceptible to perceiving these communications because they are without societal filters to dismiss or shame the experience. Among the most common experiences, especially among infants and toddlers, is an interaction with the essence of a deceased grandparent. These events may transpire through:

◈ A PLAYFUL INTERACTION WITH SOMEONE UNSEEN (THOUGH A PRESENCE MAY BE SENSED) IN WHICH THE CHILD LAUGHS OR GIGGLES; PLAYS PEEK-A-BOO-TYPE ACTIVITIES; APPEARS TO BE TICKLED; OR POINTS OR GAZES TO A SPECIFIC AREA OF THE ROOM.

◈ SIMILAR ACTIVITY OCCURRING DURING THE NIGHT, BUT THE CHILD IS WELL-RESTED THE FOLLOWING DAY, WITH NO SYMPTOMS OF SLEEPLESSNESS.

◈ VERBAL REPORTS OF SEEING GRANDMA OR GRANDPA.

◈ THE ABILITY TO IDENTIFY GRANDMA OR GRANDPA FROM FAMILY PHOTOGRAPHS, TO KNOW DETAILS OF THEIR LIVES, AND TO KNOW THEIR FIRST NAMES—DESPITE NO ONE HAVING EVER SHARED THIS INFORMATION—REGARDLESS OF WHETHER GRANDPARENT AND GRANDCHILD EVER MET.

Another common experience that shares similarities with the preceding events, and that should also be considered harmless, loving, and positive, are those in which a child appears to hold a two-way interaction or conversation with an unseen presence that some have defined as angelic. It is important, though, to distinguish this from something potentially harmful, such as the "Elliott" entity previously discussed. Positive experiences of this type may transpire through:

◈ AN INTERACTION THAT USUALLY OCCURS IN SOLITUDE AT THE SAME PLACE AND TIME WITH REGULARITY, OFTEN DAILY.

◈ AN APPARENT TWO-WAY INTERACTION, IN WHICH THE CHILD ATTENDS IN RAPT ATTENTION, AND NODS OR VERBALLY RESPONDS TO AN UNSEEN PRESENCE, AS IF ANSWERING QUESTIONS OR COMMUNICATING AN UNDERSTANDING.

◈ ANY INTERRUPTIONS BY A PARENT OR CAREGIVER TEND TO BE RESPECTFULLY IGNORED. OR THE ADULT MAY BE EXCLUDED FROM THE PROCESS BY THE CHILD (SUCH AS THE CHILD TAKING THE ADULT BY THE HAND AND ESCORTING THEM OUT OF THE ROOM), AFTER WHICH THE INTERACTION RESUMES UNTIL COMPLETE.

◈ THE CHILD EMERGES FROM THE COMPLETED INTERACTION JUBILANT, REPLENISHED, AND REFRESHED, AND JOYFULLY SEEKS TO SHARE THIS

UNDER SPIRITUAL SIEGE

SENSATION WITH OTHERS—EVEN IF IT IS UNCHARACTERISTIC TO DO SO—THROUGH PHYSICAL TOUCH AND INTIMATE INTERACTION.

These experiences may be sensed or witnessed by other family members, and tangible evidence may manifest through digital photography in which unexplainable star bursts or streaks of white light appear, or spheres of energy (or orbs) are evident. So long as these experiences are not creating anxiety and fear, there is no further intervention required.

The sensitivity or angst of children and teens may also create a vulnerability to those presences of ill-intent. Classic "noisy ghost" or poltergeist cases have typically involved this demographic as a focal point of the activity. These types of scenarios are those in which doors bang shut, pieces of furniture are tipped over, and knocking sounds may be heard. Remember that low-vibration presences thrive upon fear and chaos. Oftentimes there is friction, tension, and acute stress within the family, such as marital discord or addiction. People, especially kids and teens, may experience a haunting through:

◈ EXPERIENCING NIGHT TERRORS OR GROTESQUE NIGHTMARES.

◈ HABITUALLY AWAKENING BETWEEN MIDNIGHT AND 3:00 A.M. FEELING TERRIFIED.

◈ BECOMING INCREASINGLY ANXIOUS OR PROCRASTINATING AS BEDTIME APPROACHES, WITH COMPLAINTS ABOUT SLEEPING IN HIS OR HER OWN BEDROOM.

◈ BEING UNWILLING TO SLEEP ALONE, AND ONLY BE COMFORTED BY FALLING ASLEEP ELSEWHERE OR SLEEPING WITH FAMILY MEMBERS.

◈ REPORTING OF BLACK FIGURE-SHAPED SHADOWS, HOODED FIGURES, GHOSTLY FIGURES OR "DEMONIC" ENTITIES WITH RED EYES THAT THREATEN HARM, OR GIVE HARMFUL INSTRUCTIONS SUCH AS INCITING SELF-INJURY OR VIOLENCE AGAINST OTHERS.

◈ ACUTE HYPERACTIVITY AND ANXIETY DURING THE DAYTIME, OR AN INTENSE INCREASE IN RECKLESS OR SELF-INJURIOUS BEHAVIOR, WHICH, IF ALLOWED TO BECOME CHRONIC, MAY RESULT IN A LEGITIMATE MENTAL HEALTH DIAGNOSIS.

Other haunting symptoms may include some or all of the following:

◈ NEGATIVE EMOTIONS AND EVENTS PERPETUATE IN THE HOUSEHOLD INCLUDING DEPRESSION, FEAR, REVENGE, RAGE, ADDICTION, AND ABUSE.

◈ UNSEEN PHYSICAL MANIPULATION OR INTERFERENCE OF ELECTRICITY IN THE HOUSEHOLD, SUCH AS TVs, PHONES, AND COMPUTERS SCRAMBLING, MALFUNCTIONING, OR OPERATING INDEPENDENTLY.

- ◈ LIGHT BULBS MAY BLOW OUT FREQUENTLY OR FLICKER.
- ◈ FAMILY PETS, PARTICULARLY DOGS, MAY SEEM INCREASINGLY ANXIOUS, "CLINGY," AND IN NEED OF ATTENTION OR REASSURANCES.
- ◈ UNEXPLAINABLE COLD DRAFTS OR A PARTICULAR ROOM THAT NEVER SEEMS TO GET WARM.

In extreme cases, additional symptoms of those under siege may include:

- ◈ HUMAN-SHAPED SHADOWS OR SEEMINGLY REAL PRESENCES.
- ◈ HEARING VOICES, BREATHING, MUSIC, AND FOOTSTEPS.
- ◈ SMELLING A FOUL ODOR WITHOUT A KNOWN SOURCE.
- ◈ BEING TOUCHED, SCRATCHED, OR BITTEN.
- ◈ FEELING PINNED TO THE BED.
- ◈ OBJECTS BEING MOVED OR THROWN.
- ◈ OBJECTS DISAPPEARING AND REAPPEARING IN UNLIKELY PLACES.
- ◈ DOORS, CUPBOARDS, AND DRAWERS OPENING AND CLOSING INDEPENDENTLY.

Incredibly, my first haunting investigation had nearly *all* of the preceding symptoms. It took place in a community group home for three young men with developmental disabilities. One of them had autism and although he couldn't speak, he could type on a portable keyboard quite fluently. This gentleman was clearly being terrorized, awakening in the middle of the night shrieking in fear. He was also attacking his caregivers, grabbing them by the throat. Those who may not presume his intellectual capacity might suggest his behavior was merely a manifestation of his disability. But when someone asked him what was wrong, he typed the word "ghost."

The staff of caregivers was also experiencing very unusual activity. There were reported blasts of cold air and instances in which items were displaced, such as a stack of papers scattered across the room. One night, a little girl's voice was heard talking and giggling, and someone else saw her reflection in a window. Most dramatically, in two photographs taken of the young man with autism, faces could be seen hovering in the air near him; one face was that of a bearded man. The peculiar thing was the house wasn't that old. At the time of the investigation, the house was less than forty years old. *But* there was a small, overgrown graveyard with headstones dating to the 1800s directly adjacent to the house on the same property. When the young man with autism was calm enough to focus, he began identifying the ghosts that were plaguing him by typing out their names. There was over a half-dozen of them, and when the caregivers checked the names against the graveyard headstones, *they all matched!*

Something else aligned upon researching the names further: a number of the deceased family members died from tuberculosis, which would've caused the sensation of choking. This is precisely what the young man with autism was experiencing—and attempting to communicate—when he was grabbing people by the throat! At one point, this young man typed to me, "Love me as you love Christ. Ghosts in my room. Can't sleep. I'm scared. Help me."

What followed his heart-wrenching plea for help was a cleansing ritual in which I participated with several other psychics while the house residents and caregivers went out for the evening. I will fully explain how to enact this process in chapter seven. But if someone you know or live with is communicating to you their great discomfort, if not outright terror, over experiencing something potentially paranormal, it is important to bear in mind several principles of respect:

- ◈ Honor and acknowledge that person's experiences as their truth, no matter how far-out or unbelievable it sounds. No matter what anyone else thinks, what's happening is very real to them.

- ◈ Maintain ethics of disclosure. This means you uphold the trust someone has placed in you as a confidant by not revealing what they've shared with others without express permission to do so.

- ◈ Refrain from sensationalizing the individual's experiences. Do not magnify or embellish what is being revealed to you because it's as exciting or glamorous as a Hollywood movie. As you've read, experiencing some unseen force that can't be rationally explained and which seems bent on terrorizing a person is nerve-wracking and exhausting, and has caused many people to question their sanity.

- ◈ Take respectful measures to support the individual to feel safe. Be an emotional resource for that person by demonstrating compassion, concern, and understanding. Assist them in making the proper connections to people who can help. Nowadays, more than ever, there are religious, spiritual, and paranormal resources accessible in many communities.

In the preceding anecdote about the young man with autism who was haunted, the disruptive presences were already attached to the property. They may have been aroused by the acute sensitivity of my friend. To my knowledge, no one else who lived or worked at the property was agitating the situation through the active use of harmful drugs, pornography, or issues of violent rage. This is to suggest that in ascertaining the truth of the haunting situation, a consideration is that the present inhabitants may not have had any bearing on the circumstances, other than to simply exist in the environment; the predisposition to haunting symptoms may well have been cemented prior to the current residents' relocation.

In one such instance of this type of haunting, a client, who is also psychic, had been struggling with a series of physical health issues over a period of a year or more. As such, he was especially vulnerable for his mental, physical, and spiritual resistance being so low. In recent times, he had several upsetting experiences in his own home, including being awakened during the night by a growling presence at his bedside and feeling as though he was partially paralyzed upon awakening. I was able to intuit that above his family room there was a tear in the ethereal space there, a portal through which negative energies were entering with relative ease. I couldn't imagine that this person had done anything—consciously or unconsciously—to attract such low-frequency disruptions. However, I quickly learned that not one, but all three, of the previous owners of the house perpetuated abusive, addictive, and negative behaviors that created a predisposition to these types of energies. Indeed, the portal may have been there when my client moved in originally; but now that his mental, physical, and spiritual well-being was compromised, he came under spiritual siege. What he required to remedy this situation was the loving support of an ally to aid him to regain his ability to protect himself and preserve the sanctity of his living space.

Similar to this type of situation, it may also be that folks have unwittingly brought negative energy into their home—where previously there had been none—by virtue of acquiring an object or antique that was owned and used by someone with a highly questionable past or a vile personhood. As a result, the object has retained the hurtful energy, and introducing it into a pure environment may (but not necessarily *will*) release that energy, causing symptoms of a haunting.

One of the very best ways to support someone struggling with a haunting situation is to aid them to feel spiritually empowered to combat whatever it is that is derailing them or their family instead of feeling victimized. The next chapter is one premise for helping to build a spiritual reserve from which the person so empowered can reclaim hope and confidence in knowing they have spiritual allies on their side.

CHAPTER FIVE · UNDER SPIRITUAL SIEGE

Chapter Six

PROPER PROTECTION

In my work as a spiritual counselor and adviser I encounter all too often people who do not pray, pray inconsistently, or who don't know how to pray. A common excuse is that they "forget," like forgetting to floss or balance the check book. Some haven't thought about God, or a Higher Power, in such a long time that they feel it's useless to start praying now. Others think that going to church or temple is the only way to pray and they haven't the time. While I would never discourage anyone from participating in religious service with a congregation, it's not about a place; it's about a purpose. Please know that God is patient and always accessible to you no matter your environment or circumstances.

When I ask my clients if they have ten minutes a day for God, they all invariably say yes. But saying you will commit to the intention and actually manifesting the intention are two different things. This process will require self-discipline in order to be conscious and aware enough to make time to be with God on a daily basis. I recommend that this prayer time be the same ten minutes every day in order to develop a good habit and make the time fit within the flow of your typical daily routine. Some people choose to pray as they are awakening to a new day, others pray at bedtime, and still others pray during their lunch break. Personally, I pray throughout every day so that my conscious state becomes almost a perpetual meditation.

Here's a way to pray that I have found useful and effective. It may be used as a starting point from which to expand your good thoughts and intentions. I want for each client of mine to understand that praying isn't a quickie recitation-by-rote-and-you're-covered. Nor does prayer require great expanses of time that make it unrealistic or insurmountable. The significance of the prayer lies in the thought and emotion invested in it, not necessarily the amount of time.

Nearly everyone can relate to the metaphor of throwing a stone into a pond or lake. I use this universal experience to illustrate how to enact the prayer. As the stone pierces the surface of the water, it creates a series of concentric circles that gradually expand outward from the point of contact—we call this the "ripple effect." And so, start low and go slow by praying from smallest to largest. I encourage my clients to think of themselves as the stone by starting the prayer with what is most familiar and what they know best: themselves.

As the stone, begin the prayer not by praying for what you think you want and need but by expressing gratitude for what you already *have*. Too many of us take too much for granted. Not one of us is promised another day, let alone another moment. I recommend praying selflessly. I suggest offering appreciation and thanksgiving for all the gifts and blessings and privileges that have been bestowed upon you on this day of life.

Strip it down to the bare essentials, for example: Thank you for my eyesight to take in the beauty of all I survey. Thank you for my legs to carry me whereas others are less fortunate. (For example, in this instance, think of athletes running the 2013 Boston Marathon who lost their limbs in the blink of an eye from the explosion of bombs during a deliberate act of terrorism.) Thank you for food and fresh water to consume where such commodities are scarce for others. Thank you for employment where others are struggling. Thank you for a place to live where others haven't a place to call their own. Thank you for prosperity, which may not come in the form of money but in an exchange of goods and services. Thank you for presenting me with opportunities to be a better human being today than I was yesterday. Thank you for granting that I might employ my gifts and talents to render service to others.

These are merely a few examples of expressing gratitude. Of course, you are welcome to tailor these expressions however it best suits you.

Finally, request that divine guidance might be impressed within you to assist you in making proper decisions and to inspire you with creativity and ingenuity.

Next, the first ripple created by the stone's impact symbolizes those closest to you, perhaps those with whom you cohabitate, such as a roommate, a spouse, your parents, siblings, or your children. Pray for their health, safety and well-being. Pray that you might be of service to them. Pray that they will find the spiritual strength to manage whatever may come their way, and to respond in a manner that is right and true and good and kind.

The second ripple might include persons beyond your immediate group of loved ones, such as extended family, friends, coworkers, or neighbors. If they seem too many in number, alternate on whom you wish to focus on a given day.

The third ripple might include anyone in your community with whom you also have an emotional connection.

The fourth ripple outward from the stone is a global one that might include other human beings unknown to you but of whom you have been made aware by national or international news such as a child who had a stroke of brilliance and is making a difference in the lives of others. Or the people of a foreign nation who suffer from the daily fear and anxiety of violent warfare.

The fifth ripple may be for the souls of others whom you have known and loved and lost, or those to whom you are indebted, such as anyone who has sacrificed their lives by rendering service to others. Again, you may wish to be selective depending on how you feel guided.

The sixth ripple—and the seventh portion of the prayer—is reserved for God or your Higher Power. God bless God. God bless the angels who have been known to take human form to intervene and avert a tragedy, and then vanish without a trace. God bless every good thing that God embodies in our lives.

If this seems like too much to do or remember, begin with just the first one or two steps. Or create your own sequence based on the examples here.

Personal experience has shown me that being conscious and aware of expressing this prayer—or any similar meditation—results in attracting to me positive people and positive circumstances while minimizing the negative. This is key to creating more positive energy and less negative energy from which negative forces can perpetuate. You may also find yourself better equipped to manage a spiritual assault or other crisis by drawing upon the spiritual reserve you have established as you would make a withdrawal from a bank. I have found my altruistic appreciation is reciprocated tenfold—often when I least expect it. This doesn't happen in a manner that is grandiose but in simple, subtle ways that answer my questions or provide for my needs in the moment. I wholeheartedly believe this empowerment can manifest for you as a by-product of practicing a daily prayer. But that's not why you do it. We are spiritual beings having a human experience, and I see this prayer as one response to practicing our humanity.

In addition to thoughtful prayer and meditation, another method by which you may protect yourself is by calling upon your spirit guide. We all have at least one spirit guide—a formerly human soul assigned to be our earthly tutor to impress inspiration within us, to support us in decision making, and to collaborate with us in creative endeavors. Do you know your guide(s)? If not, here is a step-by-step process through which to engage, connect, and communicate with this nurturing and protective spiritual presence.

> **First, select a name.** Our spirit guides are typically not souls known to us in this lifetime. In order to personalize the relationship with our "spiritual cheerleaders" it is helpful to think of this presence as an ally and companion. You would call any other friend by their name, so why not your spirit guide? You can select your spirit guide's name one of two ways: impulsively or contemplatively. If impulsively, go with the very first name that pops into your head—regardless of gender (and remember that a great many names are suitable for use by both sexes). If contemplatively, you may wish to invest more time in sensing the spirit energy around you—does it feel more masculine or feminine? Are you feeling pulled to a particular name from your past, an ancestor perhaps? Or maybe the first name of someone you'd like to honor that has passed on, such as a teacher or friend? Whatever you do, select only *one* name for your guide.

> **Next, formally christen your guide.** I strongly recommend that this be done in the context of a prayer. The reason is that if you've come this far in your spiritual awakening, then you are in the act of *becoming*. As such, you are vulnerable to negative energies that desire to hinder and curtail your progress. Without protecting yourself in prayer, those negative energies may seize upon the opportunity to masquerade as something they're not in order to initiate chaos and destruction (as can happen when misusing a Ouija board). In the prayer, you may

wish to use language similar to the effect of, "For the greater good of the highest order, I christen thee _____. Please step forward to take an active role in my life as my spiritual guide and mentor. Support me in making authentic decisions, impress inspiration within me, and aid me as I move forward in service to others."

Finally, await validation from your guide. Once you've set the intention to connect with your spirit guide, and have done so with heartfelt commitment, pay attention—about a week to ten days out, you should receive validation of this new presence. You may receive only one or you may receive any number of validations in combination with one another. Here, then, are six signs of which to be aware as your spirit guide makes his or her presence known in your life:

1. The first possible sign is **validation of the name**. You have been instructed to select just one name by which to christen your spirit guide in order to make the relationship personal and palatable enough for you to relate to this unique communion. Have you encountered a manifestation of this name under unusual circumstances? For example, one young man whom I had mentored in this process was passionate about music and played guitar in a band. After meditating, he decided to call his spirit guide Roland, a fairly uncommon name. Within a week, he received a catalog in the mail addressed to him from a company with which he had never before done business. The front cover of the catalog was a close-up image of a guitar and the name of the company was printed in large letters across the top of the front cover: ROLAND. Non-believers will qualify this as mere coincidence; believers will appreciate the synchronicity of the timing, the fact that the unsolicited catalog was addressed to my friend by name, that the instrument of his musical interest was illustrated on the cover, and, of course, the affirmation of his spirit guide's name.

2. The second possible sign is a **ringing in one ear**. This ringing sensation may occur when you are in moments of high thought, contemplating spiritual questions; or it may occur when you are feeling a strong, high-vibration emotion such as happiness, compassion, and love. The ringing will be temporary and will endure for about the amount of time it takes for you to recognize its connection to what you're experiencing in the moment it occurs. For example, you might be watching or reading a news story about someone who independently takes up a cause to fundraise money in order to be of

service to those in his or her community. As the feeling of altruism and appreciation resonates within you, the ringing may begin. This is your guide confirming, "Yes, yes! Feel more of this feeling more often and employ it to serve others." The ringing should be neither unpleasant nor intrusive, as is the way of your guide. (Of course if it persists and becomes unpleasant or intrusive, seek medical advice. Your guide would not be the source of anything detrimental to your health.)

3. The third possible sign is that you may notice **an unexpected blue or white flash of light out of the corner of one eye, or you may see a sphere of spiritual energy**, commonly called an "orb." The light or orb may even travel by bobbing about or moving quickly through your space. If you engage in prayer and meditation, you may actually "see" in your mind's eye a pinpoint of light that lingers long enough for you to acknowledge its presence. The pinpoint of light may come simultaneous to your experiencing the sensation of high thought and emotion, or it may come as you are thinking about the loving and supportive presence that is your spirit guide. As before, this should not be persistent, unpleasant or intrusive; if so, please seek medical advice.

4. The fourth possible sign is that of being **aware of seeing "threes."** After naming your spirit guide, you may become increasingly aware of seeing things in sets of three. One interpretation is that this symbolizes the Holy Trinity. Most often, the threes manifest in two forms. One is seeing three creatures of the same species together, such as three ladybugs, three black crows or three bright red cardinals. The other form is seeing a sequence of the same three numbers on a digital clock, such as 1:11 or 3:33. When this occurs, and you become conscious and aware of it, pay attention to what or whom you were thinking of in the moment just prior to seeing the threes. It should be spiritually or emotionally significant.

5. The fifth possible sign is of **sensing a positive presence around you.** Another sign your spirit guide is near is that you'll feel you're not alone even when you're alone. Most often, you will experience this sensation when you are engaged in the act of creating or composing something. This is one way in which our spirit guides partner with us: to collaborate in the act of manifesting something of usefulness,

UNDERSPIRITUAL SIZE

purpose, and ingenuity. It may be that you feel guided when engaged in crafting a work of art or a musical composition; or you may receive a rejuvenation of energy or inspiration just when you need it when problem solving. If you are communicating significant concepts with others, you may find that the proper approach and phrasing of language will be "impressed" within you, granting you greater authenticity.

6. The sixth possible sign is an **increasing awareness of mentorship opportunities.** If you have come so far in your spiritual awakening as to invite the collaboration of your spirit guide, you may be prepared to receive spiritual mentorship opportunities. This may come in the form of your limits being tested, such as resisting a temptation that presents itself (where you previously would've succumbed), or better discerning right from wrong so that you extricate yourself from culpability in any wrongdoing. These opportunities will be synchronous and obvious enough for you to recognize that they were "planted" with deliberate intention to see how you'd react. Similar mentoring opportunities may manifest in dreams.

When I was engaged in the process of emerging and evolving, I began being tutored in nightly dreams. This was the perfect vehicle for me, as in dreams I was a captive audience and the unusual circumstances were completely plausible in context (as opposed to being freaked out by the same things happening in real time). In the dreams I had during this period, I was shown the despicable, degrading things people will do to themselves and to others for money. I was shown how to maximize mind over matter by opening a nightstand drawer with my thoughts. And I was with my spirit guide for the lesson in which I learned that thought equals form. In that dream, my guide was positioned above me and to the right in a room without walls, if you can imagine such a space. With his urging, and to an energetic musical accompaniment, I mentally manifested extraordinary, psychedelic bursts of colors and patterns just by letting go of self-consciousness, moving to the beat of the music, and believing in my own potential. It was amazing.

Other lessons may manifest in problem-solving situations, like the dream I had in which I was responsible for preserving a gallon of milk for a family's supper on a hot July day. In the dream, the resolution I decided upon happened when I located a workman with a cooler who allowed me to store the milk in it until needed for the family's meal. In another problem-solving dream, I was walking through my home but was expectedly blocked from entering my living room by an invisible wall that had been placed there by something nefarious. My challenge was to discern a clever solution to outwitting my nemesis and overcome the barrier in my path. I solved the problem when I made out a small chink in the wall and, transforming myself into a liquid state, I easily passed right through the hole and came out the other side. So, instead of overexerting energy to dismantle the entire wall, I merely used to my best advantage what was already in place—which, being placed there by something evil, was flawed.

None of these mentoring experiences that you may receive should be unsettling whatsoever. It is appropriate to interpret them as blessings, especially when connected to high-vibration thought or emotion. These signs your spirit guide is here are part and parcel of elevating your spiritual frequency so that you are poised to be the conduit for all that is right and true and good and kind. This will be particularly useful if you intend to lead a ritual for clearing someone's home environment of negative energy.

CHAPTER SIX

Chapter Seven

CLEARING HOUSE

If you believe you are under spiritual siege and are uncertain about your situation, or you feel ill-equipped about how to proceed, you may decide to seek assistance by consulting a psychic or similar intuitive practitioner. This person should be able to offer you valuable insight and a balanced, non-emotional perspective that will help you to determine next steps. They may also be able to identify the source of your haunting symptoms, especially if negative energy has attached to one or more people in the household. Here are some ways to determine if a psychic is legitimate and might be a resource to you.

> **Don't have too specific an agenda.** It's okay to want to know certain things as a result of your psychic session; your psychic will probably allow you to ask questions as well. But if your sole intention for booking a session is to get *the* defining answer to a specific question, you'll likely end up disappointed. The reason is that if the psychic is authentic, the information they communicate doesn't come from them, it comes *through* them. This means that the psychic has little control over what they are being spiritually guided to convey. You'll

receive what you need, not what you want—which may be two very different things. For example, you may think your sixteen-year-old son is doing fine, but the psychic may have the impression of drugs or others who use illegal substances around him. This could be the source of any negative energy that has invaded your living space.

Let the psychic guide the session. You're paying a professional psychic for his or her time; allow them to do their job and lead the discussion where it needs to go. A good psychic should do most of the talking and ask you to validate or confirm the impressions they receive. You will likely frustrate an authentic psychic with your emotional overload by going off on tangents or venting your life story. And you'll be giving a fraudulent psychic way too much information that can be manipulated to their advantage. When in doubt, politely ask the psychic if you may elaborate to underscore a point.

During your session, listen for credible details. An authentic psychic will be able to spontaneously provide you with (sometimes odd or unusual) tidbits of information to affirm that they are indeed connecting with you properly. Don't expect to hear the exact "code" word you had with your deceased cousin or the secret signal you had with your old boyfriend. In fact, just the opposite may be true. Once during a session, I felt I was connecting with a gentleman's brother who had passed on when they were younger. I kept "seeing" activities centered on a tree house, climbing trees, or jumping out of trees. The man confirmed that his brother used to always torment him by jumping out of trees to scare him when they were kids—a totally random thing. Also, be open to what is being communicated. Often people will develop "psychic amnesia," by which they become oblivious to the obvious for not having total recall in the moment. Grant that you might require process time beyond your session for recollections to surface in your memory bank.

If you feel as though there's a ghostly presence in your living environment, you'll want to know ahead of time if you are booked for a session with a psychic or a medium. All mediums are psychic, but not every psychic is a medium. A medium is someone who can willfully connect with spirits, such as one or more of your loved ones who have passed on. A psychic is someone who specializes in communicating intuitive information about your life, relationships, and your future. Find out in advance if the practitioner with whom you'd like to book a session is a psychic, a medium, or both. It will aid you in tempering your expectations.

Go in open-minded. While it's okay to have expectations of wanting to hear from a loved one, don't be surprised if your deceased alcoholic uncle who abused you when you were a kid comes through instead. This tends to be the way things work spiritually, and the communication from the uncle could very well be exactly what you're intended to receive as it pertains to healing your family and life in general.

Don't be afraid to terminate any session that doesn't feel right. No reputable psychic will ever predict your death, foretell a tragedy, give you winning lottery numbers, or inform you that you have a curse put upon you and your family and that to remove it, you need to return repeatedly. A reputable psychic will also not keep increasing their fee with each visit, or expect that you buy ancillary merchandise from them on a regular basis. Run, don't walk, from anyone who conducts business with you in a manner that does not feel authentic. On rare occasion, I may be challenged in connecting with a client. In the past ten years, this has happened about four or five times. In those situations, I will stop and ask the client how they'd like to handle it, an option of which may be to end the session at no charge to the client. An inauthentic psychic will bluff their way through for being focused on making a buck.

These principles are a good place to begin when considering a psychic reading. Don't hesitate to ask for references or to research a psychic online. Word of mouth is how I've always done business and I have received many clients as referrals from others who were satisfied customers. A good psychic's work will speak for itself.

If you elect to consult a psychic about your situation, and if he or she validates what you suspect is some sort of spiritual siege, he or she may or may not be the person to call for follow up. Just as not every psychic is a medium, not every psychic is capable of clearing house. The intuitive person whom you have consulted may simply not wish to get involved because they do not deal with negative energies or they may feel unequipped to help you directly. Your psychic may advise you to rid your living space of negative energies by burning sage or *smudging* the environment. This seems to be a fairly universal response in such instances. (I would not discourage this process but I also think it should occur in tandem with prayer.)

Most importantly, however, your psychic might be able to direct you to a person or group of people who may be able to further your understanding and possibly aid you to clear your home of negative energy because it is their area of specialty. If this person cannot recommend anyone to you, simply conduct an Internet search for "paranormal investigation" in your vicinity.

Please know that investigating alleged hauntings is a hobby or avocation for many paranormal investigation teams, so be patient for a reply to your phone call or email. This also means that the team may not be able to address your concerns with the immediacy you would wish. (Understandably, if you believe you and your family are under spiritual assault, you want it taken care of as soon as possible!)

This is very much a burgeoning field. There is no licensing or certification that is universally recognized. While they may be in contact with other groups, paranormal investigation teams are self-contained and governed by their own individual code of ethics. Legitimate paranormal investigation teams typically do not charge for their services. While they should uphold confidentiality about your case, they may ask your permission to share the circumstances of your situation (anonymously if you choose) with other teams or post the case to their Web site.

The proper approach for a paranormal investigation team is that of a scientific and analytical position in seeking a logical or natural explanation for what you are experiencing. They may bring with them various kinds of equipment to conduct their investigation. Some paranormal investigation teams may also bring a psychic or a medium with them to aid in corroborating their findings or to offer historical clues for further investigation.

You will be interviewed for an initial assessment and will likely be involved during the investigation so that you can answer questions or affirm any findings. (If you are asked to be videotaped, you should be able to decline without recourse; if you agree, there should be a photo release form acknowledging and limiting the use of your image.) The paranormal investigation team should keep you closely informed, address all of your questions as honestly and as completely as possible, and should share their findings with you in a timely manner.

The paranormal investigation team should not have as its goal confronting or provoking any alleged presence in your home—which may only make things worse after they leave! Nor should they be primarily focused on capturing audio or video evidence in order to sensationalize it or enhance their reputation in the field. A legitimate paranormal team should not make you feel worse about your situation by overemphasizing, exaggerating, or emotionally embellishing the circumstances. (If you are truly under spiritual siege, you don't want to be told—or overhear—comments such as, "This is so much worse than we thought!") They should also not make you feel as though you are being accused or blamed for your situation. Their approach should be one of educating and empowering you. The communication among the team members should make you feel as though you are a valued participant and not excluded as a bystander at the mercy of their outcome.

The paranormal investigation team may or may not be able to directly provide you with a solution to remedy your circumstances. They are primarily there to offer their para-professional evaluation as to whether your experience is a legitimate haunting or if there are other explanations such as natural causes or, in some instances, the attention-seeking behavior or mental-emotional issues of a family member.

The concept of demonic possession was most spectacularly portrayed in *The Exorcist* but has gained in popularity in a spate of recent horror films dealing with this subject matter. There is dissension about what constitutes a true case of possession versus undiagnosed mental illness. Some of the symptoms of both circumstances crosswalk from one to another, such that one wonders if both experiences aren't interconnected one to the other in a vicious cycle. Where the Catholic Church is concerned, exorcism is not a subject taken lightly, and reportedly most dioceses have an exorcist trained to perform the rites necessary to relieve a victim of demonic possession. No one reading this should attempt to self-diagnose a case of demonic possession without seeking spiritual or religious intervention and support. Some of the symptoms that constitute a case of possession are:

❖ A SIGNIFICANT CHANGE FROM THE INDIVIDUAL'S "NORMAL" PERSONALITY TO ONE OF RAGE AND ABUSIVE BEHAVIOR.

❖ A CHANGE IN THE PERSON'S VOICE—IN SOUND AND TONE.

❖ THE PERSON HAVING LITTLE OR NO APPETITE.

❖ ACTS OF SELF-MUTILATION SUCH AS BITING, SCRATCHING, OR CUTTING ONE'S FLESH.

❖ DISTORTIONS IN THE PERSON'S POSTURE AND FACIAL EXPRESSIONS.

- ❖ THE PERSON HAVING UNUSUAL STRENGTH BEYOND THEIR AGE OR USUAL PHYSICAL CAPABILITIES.
- ❖ THE PERSON IS FLUENT IN A PREVIOUSLY UNLEARNED LANGUAGE OR THEY UNDERSTAND A FOREIGN LANGUAGE.
- ❖ THE PERSON HAVING KNOWLEDGE OF INFORMATION NOT PREVIOUSLY KNOWN TO THEM.
- ❖ THE PERSON'S ABILITY TO FORETELL FUTURE EVENTS.
- ❖ THE SENSATION OF SIGNIFICANT CHILL IN THE PERSON'S ROOM.
- ❖ OBJECTS LEVITATE OR MOVE IN PROXIMITY TO THE PERSON.
- ❖ THE PERSON VOMITS UNUSUAL OBJECTS OR OTHERWISE INEDIBLE ITEMS.
- ❖ THE PERSON HAS A VIOLENT REACTION TO RELIGIOUS OBJECTS OR SYMBOLS.
- ❖ THE PERSON IS INSENSITIVE OR VIOLENT WHEN ENTERING A CHURCH OR HEARING QUOTES FROM THE BIBLE. HE OR SHE CANNOT TOLERATE HEARING THE NAME JESUS CHRIST.

In nearly all cases of a haunting, the first response is to seek outside support and assistance to eradicate the problem. Depending on one's background, an initial reaction may be to contact one's church or synagogue and arrange to have the affected environment blessed. This approach should never be discouraged, and having one's home blessed can also occur in tandem with a paranormal team investigation. But know that oftentimes such a blessing doesn't "take," or things will improve for a couple weeks and return right back to where it started (or even worsen). The reason for this is that the individual conducting the religious ceremony does not have a personal and emotional investment in your home. But *you* do! And, ultimately, the responsibility for the maintenance and upkeep of the spiritual-emotional climate of your household falls to you and everyone living under the same roof. Moving away may seem like a logical choice, but it is not necessarily a solution either (nor a very practical one). If negative energies have attached to toxic or vulnerable personalities in the environment, they can follow you to the next place.

Knowledge is power, and this chapter will close with a protocol to address the personal responsibility incumbent upon you if you are under spiritual siege and wish to make it better. The next chapter will outline a process by which you can continue on a path toward emerging and evolving into an improved version of your old self. This will also allow you to shed any aspect of your personhood which is inauthentic, thereby empowering you with spiritual resiliency and confidence.

One thing you should know is that when things seem dormant, the dark energy—be it a bitter ghost or a demonic presence—tends to gravitate to the deepest, darkest area of the building, be it a crawl space or a basement. It is here that little or no light gets in to illuminate the truth. Oftentimes, this dark energy will lurk in a far corner, behind a furnace or hot water heater, for example. Once when investigating a haunting, I led a prayer circle in which the residents of the home and I joined hands and prayed. We were in the blackest area of the basement and I turned my back to a room with no electricity to light it. As I led the prayer, I sensed something absolutely monstrous in size rise up behind me. Distracted, I momentarily lost my place—which is precisely what the presence wanted, to cause me to become undone. A colleague with me sensed this as well and squeezed my hand, which brought me "back," and I was able to proceed. If you are remotely Christian, I also strongly advise invoking the name Jesus Christ. It is not enough to run out and purchase crucifixes or figurines; there needs to be a spiritual and emotional investment in the power these items symbolize. Personally, I am non-denominational Christian but I have seen imps scatter to the four corners of the room when I enter because they know full well who I am there representing, full of compassion for the afflicted family. Once when I walked into a teenage boy's bedroom, which looked like a cyclone hit it, something jumped out the second-story window screaming like a cat that had been scalded. Again, it knew full well who I was there representing. *You* also have this capacity to rid yourself of evil or negative influences, if not through Jesus Christ, then through the power of love within a family united.

The sole antidote to counteract presences of ill-intent is LOVE. Love is a high-vibration emotion that will diffuse negative, low-vibration emotions such as hate, revenge, jealousy, self-loathing and so on. Therefore, you are encouraged to identify family stressors that may perpetuate low-vibration emotions. Are there toxic issues within yourself or others that need to be illuminated and eliminated, if not contained? It is also a time to assess family faith and spirituality. You may, at this time, recommit to attending religious service; however, this is not about praying or practicing your faith in a *place*; it's about a recommitment to being conscious and aware of what that faith signifies on a regular, if not daily, basis.

Here is a protocol to consider consistently implementing with as many members of your household as are willing to participate (which will hopefully be all):

- ❖ ESTABLISH A CLEAR, CONSISTENT, AND PREDICTABLE SCHEDULE FOR BRINGING CLOSURE TO THE DAY'S ACTIVITIES AS A FAMILY WHERE POSSIBLE.
- ❖ USE BATH TIME AS AN OPPORTUNITY TO DE-STRESS AND CALM, FOR CHILDREN ESPECIALLY. USE SOFT LIGHTING, FAVORED MUSIC, AND SCENTED BATH WATER (LAVENDER IS PARTICULARLY SOOTHING).
- ❖ GATHER TOGETHER AS A FAMILY OVER A MEAL TO DISCUSS THE DAY'S EVENTS AND REINFORCE THE UNITY OF THE FAMILY BONDED IN LOVE AND SUPPORT OF ONE ANOTHER.
- ❖ AS PART OF THIS DISCUSSION, VALIDATE EACH OTHER'S PLACE AND ROLE IN THE FAMILY, AND WHAT EACH PERSON CONTRIBUTES TO THE UNITY OF THE FAMILY UNIT.
- ❖ JOIN IN PRAYER OR MEDITATION.
- ❖ BLESS THE HOUSE, PARTICULARLY THE BEDROOM OF ANYONE WHOSE SLEEP HAS BEEN DISTURBED.
- ❖ PRAY FOR THE INDIVIDUAL PROTECTION OF EACH PERSON AFFECTED.
- ❖ PRAY FOR THE UNWANTED PRESENCES, WHICH WILL CONFUSE AND DISARM THEM. DIRECT THEM INTO THE GLORIOUS WHITE LIGHT WHERE THEY WILL BE WELCOMED AND RECEIVED, REDEEMED AND REJUVENATED.
- ❖ EMPOWER EACH FAMILY MEMBER WITH THE AUTHORITY TO DRAW STRENGTH FROM HIS OR HER FAITH TO COMMAND THE UNWANTED PRESENCES TO LEAVE.
- ❖ MAKE THIS TANGIBLE FOR CHILDREN BY PROVIDING THEM WITH A FLASHLIGHT, SQUIRT-GUN, OR RELIGIOUS OBJECT TO WARD OFF NIGHTTIME INTERRUPTIONS.
- ❖ MAKE EACH BEDROOM AS PLEASING AN ENVIRONMENT AS POSSIBLE WITH ATTENTION TO BEDDING FABRICS, LIGHTING OR NIGHT-LIGHTS, AND SOOTHING MUSIC OR PEACEFUL SOUNDS (SUCH AS A GENTLE RAIN SHOWER OR OCEAN WAVES PLAYED ON A RECORDING).
- ❖ KNOW THAT LOVE WITHIN A FAMILY UNITED WILL CREATE MORE AND MORE POSITIVE EMOTION THAT WILL BENEFIT THE ENTIRE FAMILY, CREATING LESS AND LESS NEGATIVE EMOTION, WHICH FEEDS THE SPIRITUAL ASSAULT.

To bless the house, gather together anyone over the age of thirteen (it is best to exclude impressionable young children unless they are mature and capable of participating). From top to bottom, in every bathroom and every closet, join hands in a circle. Whomever wishes to begin should say a prayer of love and protection. Each member of the circle is encouraged to make a contribution to the prayer with heartfelt thoughts, words, and feelings. Here is a sample prayer to consider using:

Heavenly Father, author of the Universe and Creator of all that is seen and unseen. We are grateful, blessed, and privileged to be gathered in your holy presence. We ask that you join us in sanctifying this space and illuminating every corner with the light of the truth. Shield us in your glorious white light and repel anything that is not for our greater good. Amen.

As you become more comfortable with the process, you may use similar such language or create prayers of your own with other family members contributing to their composition. You may wish to enact this process of blessing your home weekly until you feel as though the ritual can be faded because the haunting symptoms have ceased. However, it is advised that you maintain the preceding protocol to preserve the integrity and revision of the household energy in a way that is loving, light, and positive.

Chapter Eight

SEVEN STEPS FOR SPIRITUAL WELLNESS

The world as we know it is at risk of devolving. In February 2015, respected physicist Stephen Hawking declared that human aggression was, in his opinion, the greatest threat to the longevity of humanity. Addressing a gathering at the London Science Museum, Hawking called for people to aspire to empathy in order to find peace and togetherness. Unfortunately, it should come as no surprise to anyone that ill-mannered and rude behavior has become the norm by today's standards. As one who is exquisitely sensitive, I can recall as a child being rattled for hours afterward if I overheard someone curse in anger. In fact, I was taught never to swear in front of a lady. (No one ever told me what to do if it was the lady who was swearing!) Disregard and disrespect for others is commonplace, I regret. I see it every time someone tosses a cigarette butt out of a moving car on the highway, or wastes too much food, or remains silent when a cashier gives back too much change.

When I scan the obituaries in my local paper, I see how carefully people's lives have been recounted and, oftentimes, lauded. But I don't believe that everyone who dies is a good person, free from bigotry and prejudice, and absent of selfish or vindictive conduct. (Revisit the discussion of ghosts to understand why some of these very people lag behind after death.)

I find it curious that such citizens condemn and criticize others so carelessly and then wonder why they attract misery. It sounds clichéd, but if only they understood that you get back what you put out; and that everything matters—every word, every gesture, every deed in every encounter throughout every day matters! Yet when tragedy strikes or a catastrophe occurs, it is then that these very people turn to God, pleading for their prayers to be answered with utmost urgency.

But our relationship with God is just that: a relationship built upon faith, trust, and mutual respect—the same as any other relationship that matters to us. It is a partnership that is intended to be reciprocal, meaning that, just like a true ally, God will honor our relationship if we honor Him in return. In so doing, we have a responsibility to conduct ourselves with grace and dignity to the best of our ability. I never believed the whole "why do bad things happen to good people?" paradigm because, in my opinion, the "good people" usually aren't so good. Now, I tend to be rather rigid and literal, I'll confess, and I don't expect everyone to be perfect (we wouldn't be human otherwise). But I do expect courtesy, and I am losing patience with the hypocritical and duplicitous behavior of the so-called good people.

A couple of years ago, a young couple in their twenties, engaged to be married, was killed in a car accident that was believed to have been an act of road rage. They were allegedly run off the road by a truck driver. The story made front-page news in my hometown paper and their families grieved for the matrimony that was not to be. Through events I do not recollect, the investigation revealed that they were rear-ended after giving the truck driver "the finger," which raised his ire in the moment and caused him to react rashly. Did the young couple deserve to die? Of course not. But were they truly as "good" as others claimed? And if they both found it acceptable to flash an obscene gesture at a stranger, then in what other ways did they condone or rationalize their misbehavior under other circumstances?

Pledging to renew our relationship with God requires introspection—remember, it's a partnership. Every corner of our personhood must be illuminated. There can be no secrets in this relationship, and our shortcomings and transgressions must be confronted with clarion authenticity. It requires practice and commitment on a daily basis. This process raises our consciousness *and* our conscience. Once we clean our inner "house," God becomes a God of constancy, not a God of convenience; and the relationship yields unlimited possibilities.

As I was emerging and evolving in my spirituality, I was unable to find anyone who was willing to sit with me and talk through the very unusual circumstances I was undergoing. In short, I had to figure it all out on my own and am now completely self-taught in all of my psychic work and the classes I teach. But I don't wish for anyone reading this who possesses the empathy Dr. Hawking calls for to feel as if they, too, are free-falling without a net or at least without an understanding ally. I have compartmentalized my spiritual growth into seven steps I undertook to evolve into a better person. Depending upon your personality or degree of commitment, you may wish to embark upon the path of exploring all seven steps simultaneously or one at a time. In any event, this procedure will empower you to resist and rebuke negative spiritual energies as well as empower you to feel spiritually confident moving forward.

1. The first step is to **commit to a Higher Power**. Please pause to reflect on the miraculous essence of your very being. Acknowledge your place in the Universe and recognize that you are entitled to the space that you occupy. Our culture is obsessed with physical perfection, plastic surgery, and makeovers. I recommend that you engage with the Source of Creation by celebrating your unique diversity, whether it be your unusual name, heritage, or the feature or features that make you distinct from anyone else. This uniqueness will be of service to you as you evolve spiritually because any ethereal communications you perceive will be channeled through you as the sole proprietor of your own individuality. Therefore, also pause to reflect upon and assess your gifts and talents.

You may already be aware of some of your gifts and talents because they define how you spend your free time or what you'd term a hobby or avocation; others may determine how you earn a living. But we all also have *spiritual* gifts and talents. In what ways might you be able to draw upon the intuitive, perceptive aspect of your personhood in order to reawaken dormant or suppressed thoughts, feelings, or ideas that you may have felt as a child?

2. The second step is to **be conscious and aware of the importance of daily prayer and meditation**. This is not about getting back in the habit of attending a house of worship; although, again, that should never be discouraged. This isn't about a *place*, it's about reclaiming the temple in your heart. From this, all authentic spiritual growth will emanate. If this is something you don't do, do sporadically, or haven't done since childhood, start low and go slow by beginning with a few minutes as day, as has been previously recommended. In order to develop a good habit and be consistent about maintaining it, designate the *same* few minutes each day (or longer if you can manage it).

Pray selflessly—in other words, no winning lottery numbers! Again, instead of praying for what you think you want and need, start by praying for what you *already have*. If you are unsure of where to begin, strip it down to the most fundamental essentials such as your eyesight, employment, food to eat, fresh water to drink, a place to live, people that care for you and so on—things that we may very well take for granted for being so preoccupied by our wants or blind-sided by our hectic lives. And while you shouldn't pray to win the lottery, you *can* state your intentions for where you'd like to be and what you'd like to be doing with the request that you be fairly compensated for being of service to others in the capacity of your vision. You may also ask for further guidance, direction, or resolution in dreams.

If you can devote more time to this state of solitude, see if you can expand your consciousness and stretch your imagination with visualization exercises in which you envision yourself in the future, manifesting your true heart's calling. Don't hold back for fearing your own imagination; After all, the chair upon which you are seated originated in someone's imagination. It is your birthright to create in reality what you dream for yourself.

3. It may sound clichéd, but the third step is to **practice random acts of kindness**. Have you ever watched an episode of *The Jerry Springer Show*? If not, you now have a homework assignment. The kind of insensitive, goading, name-calling, verbally-and-physically aggressive behavior demonstrated on this and a host of other reality television programs has become the mentality mindset of our culture because *people emulate what they see*. This has not only led to such behavior becoming acceptable as mainstream misconduct, it contributes to the erosion of the good and altruistic works of others who care about being respectful, gracious, and civilized. Hopefully you are (or soon will be)

among those in the latter faction. If so, please consider approaching each encounter with another human being as an *opportunity*. Position yourself so that you may be of service to others on a daily basis by being a good listener, demonstrating common courtesy and good manners, or committing an act of anonymous kindness without the idea of receiving praise or recognition for it. Take it a step further throughout each day by silently blessing or praying for the wellness of others you witness as less fortunate than yourself. The good thoughts and positive energies you exert *matter* and will have a proactive influence on the world at large as well as in your personal life.

4. Step four may present a challenge if its tenets have not been a priority: **holistic health**. For some, enacting this step will be a process. It may even be helpful to enlist the support of a trusted ally for gentle yet constructive criticism, because this step requires introspection. Begin with a broad assessment of your overall lifestyle to include an examination of the food you consume, your amount of proper rest, exercise, work, and relationships. Endeavor to clear your life of elements that can deaden or "block" you and craft a plan to address these issues. This may include personal or external pessimism, unhealthy diet, drugs, nicotine, alcohol, or pornography. Unhealthy habits will prevent you from tapping into your spiritual gifts and talents to your full potential because you need to be operating with as clean and pure and clear a channel as possible. You cannot be that authentic channel and also be the person who is cynical or sarcastic, who plays violent video games, or who watches porn in which people do degrading things to themselves and others for money or "fame." As part of this assessment process, determine how you deal with stress and negativity, especially if you have a vulnerability to relapse into an unhealthy habit under pressure. This is precisely what negative energies want: to prey upon your Achilles' heel in order to erode your well-being and impose an agenda of self-destruction. Are you able to view your areas of weakness objectively as an outsider looking in, instead of subjectively because you take it personally? Can you frame this assessment as a learning experience?

Finally, examine what you "put out there" in terms of how you interact with others. Do you aspire to conduct yourself with grace, humility, fairness, and harmless forms of humor? Or are you prone to gossip, lying, and duplicity? Language matters, and while some people say swearing is "only words," it's the *emotion* behind the intent of the words that matters. Curse words are often used in anger or to belittle or humiliate others. Recently, I was waiting for a friend to come out of a Walmart and watched as two young women exited the store. One of them was complaining and every other word she used to vent was "f*ck." I knew this wasn't an exception; this was the rule of her everyday misconduct. I could literally feel the poison seeping off of her and knew that her life was miserable. Work toward eliminating profanity from your vocabulary.

5. Step five is to **develop a regard for nature by recognizing that every new day is a gift**—none of us is guaranteed another. So offer up your heartfelt gratitude for all of nature that abounds around you by paying attention to all you survey. Be grateful for inclement weather so that we have balance in order to better appreciate beautiful days. Allow fresh air to fill your lungs and relish it—it's a gift. Every day connect with the sky, stars, trees, flowers, plants, gardens, and all living creatures. This will also grant you a heightened perspective for the first step, which is committing to a Higher Power, by recognizing the exquisite delicacy and divine wisdom by which all of nature—yourself included—has been designed. If you can walk, jog, or run on a regular basis, go outdoors to do so instead of using an indoor treadmill. You can also use this opportunity for your prayer and meditation time. And, as part of the ritual for expressing thanksgiving, you can also use this time to give thanks for the glory and magnificence of all you survey in nature.

6. The sixth step is to **prepare for visualizing how to invite prosperity into your life**. It begins with a challenging procedure: mentally reconciling your past transgressions against others. This requires that we confront the three most powerful words any of us can say about ourselves: "I was wrong." But it is the liberation of acknowledging and accepting responsibility for the ways in which we've slighted and wronged others that will elevate our spiritual consciousness. To the very best of your recollection, mentally atone for the words and misdeeds you have perpetrated in the past, the side effects of which have caused others unintentional or deliberate harm. There is no shame in confessing these egregious errors, only a heightened awareness for moving forward with the edification of not desiring to repeat such mistakes. It is a cleansing progress of self-examination and self-assessment. As part and parcel of such, you should also be able to chart your growth on a learning curve of improvement. For

example, I have known someone since the early 1980s, someone who at that time I thought was a friend. This person has a history of predatory, duplicitous, and destructive conduct. This person's narcissism has hurt many people; but, perhaps what's worse is that in all that time, this person has not evolved into a superior version of his old self. Instead, he perpetuates the same pattern of behavior without seeming to have learned or advanced because he justifies his misdeeds as being "all part of the game." It is crucial not to become "stuck" or stagnant spiritually in so pathetic a manner as this but to, instead, always be in a state of evolution toward enlightenment. It is probably best to enact this process of self-evaluation over a period of time as opposed to reviewing it all at once, which could be overwhelming and even depressing.

Once you've identified the inauthentic aspects of your personhood that you will be discarding, begin a similar process for tabulating the ways you've benefited others as well (especially to provide some balance if you're feeling like you beat yourself up!). In what ways have you been kind, generous, or altruistic without the expectation of being recognized or reciprocated? From this point on, determine and prepare to move forward in order to be of service to others in some manner *each day*. This can range from paying a compliment to the stranger in line ahead of you at the grocery store to giving away as a gift something you have created.

Now you will be poised to pray or meditate for prosperity—not necessarily wealth—to be fairly compensated for your good works. This can look like an increase in salary, shifting to a position that will make better use of your gifts and talents, or a good old-fashioned exchange of goods and services from one to another, as in bartering with a neighbor. Manifest your destiny by visualizing where you'd like to be and what you'd like to be doing in order to serve others. Pray and meditate for guidance from your spiritual allies, which leads directly into the seventh and final step.

7. The last step of this process is to **acknowledge your spiritual guardians, mentors and protectors**. Offer praise and gratitude for the protection and learning experiences you've received, much of which may have been brought to light through your personal self-assessment. Recognize those times a Higher Power intervened in your life and give praise and thanksgiving for it. A woman who took a class I offered on developing your personal intuition told of one

such event that was a turning point in her comprehension of this concept. The incident occurred while she was in college. One day she was driving along the highway with the windows open and some important school papers blew away. She pulled to the shoulder of the road, stopped the car, and started back down the highway to gather up the papers. As she turned to head back, her car exploded in a ball of fire. If it hadn't been for the nuisance of retrieving the papers, she would've been killed then and there. You may not have experienced anything quite so spectacular but you must realize the significance of acknowledging that you have partners and collaborators capable of divine intervention.

As was previously discussed, also recognize that spiritual communications can be symbolic and impressed within dreams or through creative inspiration. Finally, as was also outlined, personalize your guardians, mentors, and protectors in a manner that grants you a sense of comfort in knowing you can access these spiritual resources at will.

This protocol for attaining spiritual well-being has allowed me to develop my spiritual gifts and talents in order to provide intuitive guidance and direction for others that is authentic and usually accurate. You will also grow in a feeling of spiritual resiliency and empowerment, and this will aid you in your role as an agent of change, a catalyst to transform the lives of others, especially those under spiritual siege.

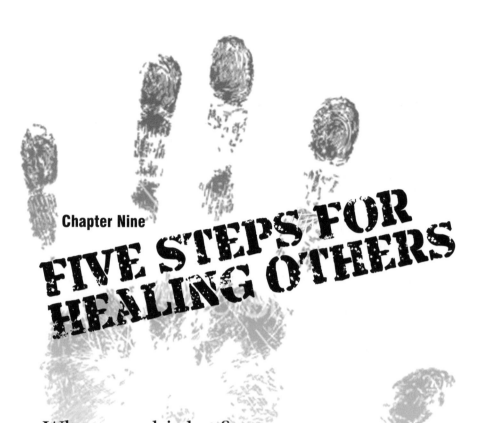

Chapter Nine

FIVE STEPS FOR HEALING OTHERS

When we think of the ability to spiritually heal others of their physical pain and discomfort, we may have thoughts of prayer or laying on of hands or perhaps alternative modalities such as Reiki, which is the practice of replenishing the body's seven energy centers, or *chakras*. I am not a Reiki master, nor do I attend a church; however, I am open to all religious and spiritual beliefs that hold reverence and honor for a Higher Power. I am self-taught but desire to share the wisdom I've been granted with others in order to create a ripple effect. The challenge is that we may tend to think that such healing capability is reserved for those of an elevated spiritual status, such as saints or those of devout religious standing. But I am here to tell you that we *all* hold the ability to relieve others of their physical pain and discomfort. Oftentimes, those who are experiencing spiritual siege are under great emotional duress that begins to affect one's physical well-being, resulting in a variety of uncomfortable or painful ailments that can cause the affected individual to become undone. This may make the individual increasingly vulnerable and weak because his or her physical resistance is low.

In order to harness the authority vested in you to root out another's source of physical pain and remove it, it will be necessary, in my opinion and in my experience, to embrace the following five principles:

1. The first principle is to **acknowledge that you will be working in concert with a Higher Power**. Therefore, enacting the healing procedure does not come from you; it comes *through you*. Remove your ego from the equation by focusing on being of compassionate good service to someone in need without the thought of recognition or compensation. And please respect that you will be channeling spiritual energy with your body serving as the spiritual conduit. Think of water running into and through a garden hose from a spigot and flushing out the other end; you are the metaphoric hose. In my opinion and in my experience, this process cannot occur without the humility of acknowledging that the ability to heal emanates from the Higher Power.

2. The second principle is to **acknowledge that you have the power to heal**. Once you have embraced the first principle, it is also important to build a spiritual reserve of confidence in knowing that the Higher Power desires you to fulfill your birthright as a human being, and that you are, indeed, fully capable of doing this. If it helps, here's my take on the secret meaning of life: we all hold the capacity to render service to others through the employ of all that we have been, all that we are presently, and all that we are becoming. Our challenge is to discern how to make the best use of who we are and then *do* what we *are* in order to help others.

3. The third principle is to **be a clear channel**. In order to properly receive and direct the healing energy that will flow through you, it is important to present with as clear and clean and pure a channel as possible. As was discussed previously, if there are vices and addictions blocking you up and affecting your mental-emotional or physical well-being, it could affect the effectiveness of the healing treatment you deliver. Assess what you are consuming and consider if your "garden hose" is being blocked by toxins such as unhealthy foods, alcohol, illegal or prescription drugs, and so on. Your positive attitude and proper physical health are imperative to the process and its success.

4. The fourth principle is to **pray with love and compassion**. Prior to entering into healing mode, it is important to pray in order to feel spiritually grounded, confident, and resilient. Pray for the protection

of yourself, especially if you'll be laying hands on someone who is emotionally, physically, and spiritually blocked (you won't wish to invite their negative energy to transfer to, and affect, you). And pray to render good and great service to the other person through all that is right and true and good and kind. The procedure for spiritual healing is not rocket science. Love and compassion for others is the conductor through which the Higher Power can most effectively operate through you.

5. The fifth principle is to **understand and acknowledge that some people won't be healed**. In your healing journey, you will encounter others who may tell you they desperately desire to be healed. But, in fact, they don't want to be healed at all. The affected person has a responsibility to cooperate with you in the process by contributing high thought and honorable prayer to the healing procedure. If the person portrays themselves as a victim or expects pity (which is different from empathy), you may find yourself stymied. For some, physical pain and discomfort has become their sole identity and social life; it brings them attention from others (family and friends as well as physicians and clinicians) and it makes them feel special. The notion of removing those aspects of their life may be threatening enough for them to resist and only pretend to go through the motions.

Next, here is the actual process by which I have been blessed to relieve others of physical pain and discomfort. In my experience, if someone has a chronic pain which they have endured over a significant period of time, the healing I can offer numbs the pain for approximately twenty-four hours, like a temporary shot of anesthesia (and for those in pain, a twenty-four-hour reprieve may be a welcome gift). If this is the case, the process may be repeated as often as you are physically and emotionally able; but be advised that it is draining and you must care for yourself first and foremost before you can be of service to others. If someone has a recent pain of about seventy-two hours or less, the pain may be eliminated altogether.

After washing your hands and clearing your mind of your own personal clutter, have the other person lie prone if they can, or at least seated comfortably. Next, identify the location of the pain on their body. Say a prayer with the person and suggest that they relax as best as they can and have them imagine an ocean with waves continuously lapping at the shoreline.

UNDER SPIRITUAL SIEGE

While the person is in a meditative state, gently place both hands directly on the affected area. If the person does not wish to be touched or it would be painful for him or her to be touched, simply place your hands in the air slightly above the affected area. If you are placing your hands directly on the person, I have found skin on skin contact is best. Now, imagine seeing the "inside" of the affected area and with your hands scoop out the black "gunk" that is the root of the pain. The black gunk is a toxic jelly-like substance that will not harm you as you are already spiritually protected.

You can dispose of the black gunk by casting it aside and directing it to a place where it will be transformed into something positive. Next, "rinse" your hands off in an imaginary stream that flows next to you. The stream is crystal clear, and its waters are both cleansing and purifying. In fact, you may decide this is the most ideal place in which to dispose of the black gunk while simultaneously rinsing off your hands. Repeat this process until you intuitively sense that you have cleared the affected area thoroughly.

After you feel you have removed the black gunk, fill the hollow area with a green healing light that you imagine flowing down your arms and out through your fingertips. At this point in the process, it would not be uncommon for you to feel a presence behind you or to feel as though the process is being facilitated by a third party. If you have properly prepared and protected yourself, there is no need to be afraid.

You can enact this process for as long as you like, but be very mindful of not causing harm to yourself. I recommend that you set a time limit for yourself initially. One of the first times I did this for someone else, it was to revive the circulation in someone's feet. I was feeling just fine during the procedure and was busily engaged with scooping out black gunk and infusing the person's feet with green healing light. The person's feet got toasty-warm and their color actually improved. I must have been doing this for close to an hour until I felt I was finished. But upon rising to my feet, I felt dizzy and had to sit down, nearly incapacitated and drained.

Now the healing procedure typically takes me about twenty minutes. The other person may feel a tingling sensation or may feel "heat" or coolness on the affected area. They should feel some measure of relief.

If there are not immediate results, do not be discouraged from continuing your good efforts. It may be that the affected person won't be aware of their relief until a short time afterwards. Or it may be that you need to repeat the process. Also be mindful of setting limits; in other words, don't succumb to flattery and create a healing "junkie" who relies on you instead of taking their own proactive and preventive measures to be well.

Chapter Ten
WHAT NEXT?

As you have read, it is a rather facile process for negative and ill-intended energies to attack those of us who are most vulnerable or unaware, such as children and teenagers and those who struggle with issues of mental wellness and addiction. These draining energies have the ability to affect our emotional well-being, our conduct, our relationships, and our ability to be productive contributors to our respective jobs and communities.

It is important to identify how to proactively practice your spirituality on a regular—if not daily—basis. For me, it is my daily walks. For others, it may be engaging in yoga, reading enlightening information, drawing or painting, or spending time in stimulating thought. As was previously discussed, this is a good opportunity for self-examination; to review the past, acknowledge the present, and dream for the future. You may also use this state of solitude to request forgiveness for having inflicted pain on others unaware. Taking steps to correct personal misconduct and that of others contributes to the good fight that is spiritual warfare. This kind of mindfulness creates an awareness and an upraised consciousness that will keep negative energies disempowered from attempting to influence or control you. But it is a choice.

You can be tempted and drawn to dark things that promise inauthentic power. If you engage those energies, they *will* reciprocate, and if you remain unaware, it may be too late when you realize you've been deceived for being so deep into a destructive relationship that has brought damage upon yourself and harmed others. Or, you can decide to engage in a relationship with a Higher Power in which you can place trust and hope, by which you are loved and adored, and through which a calling will reinforce that you are entitled to the space that you occupy for being the keeper of gifts and talents that will benefit others. This is the choice between being a selfish, angry, and unfulfilled person or an individual who maintains a spiritual toolbox that enables her to repel, rebuke, and resist negative energies.

If the information in this book resonates, and you are feeling awake and empowered, you may also feel inspired to "do something" productive with those feelings. If you feel a strong desire to carve out a formal niche by contributing actively, you might volunteer for a charity that calls to you. You may mentor someone who is enduring struggles that you once did. Or you might align yourself with human rights causes. You may even wish to join a paranormal investigation team, so long as it is for the proper and authentic reasons and not for the sensation of thrill-seeking.

Or, you might consider an inside-out approach, beginning where you are and gently influencing those in your immediate vicinity. Discover your passion and recover your creative or artistic talents with the idea of benefitting others. Use social media in a proactive manner by creating positive spiritual messages on YouTube or in a blog, so that what you have to share receives broad exposure. Advocate for yourself and others. There is extraordinary power in telling your story; it will relieve you of the burden and will have a direct spiritual impact on the lives of others. Remember: illuminating every corner of your personhood, and denying harbor to secrets of any kind, grants less and less opportunity for any negative energy to seize hold.

Another step to consider is how to avoid toxic personalities that may cause peer pressure for expecting you to become involved in harmful activities. (This may be challenging if the toxic personality is within your own family.) It is important to disallow yourself from being mistreated or abused; this isn't about martyrdom. Rebuke any form of behavior that is disrespectful and humiliating to others or yourself. Some relationships are simply not intended to be salvaged.

When you know you are going to be in the company of a person whom you consider to be a toxic individual, surround and protect yourself in an invisible, impenetrable shield of glorious white light that will resist anything negative. Do this in the context of a prayer prior to being the environment in which you anticipate encountering this person. Another strategy is to smile slightly but kindly and greet him or her by looking them directly in the eye, not in a manner than is confrontational or condescending but with the confident approach of someone who is spiritually aware and sees the grand scheme. This tactic usually disarms the person who is not at peace within themselves.

If, under the circumstances, you find that you are a captive audience, try an experiment: for each complaint you hear, respond by reversing it proactively. See if "flipping" it causes a shift of attitude in the other party. For example, if someone openly complains about bad weather, don't agree with them. Instead, remind them that it is only temporary; that the forecast calls for a great weekend; or that others living elsewhere are enduring much worse conditions. I, personally, have done this on occasion, and it's fascinating to see how others slowly transform, unaware of what is occurring. This is because we all intrinsically know that the right thing to do is to be good and kind and decent. Your behavior will be the model after which others will pattern their own conduct.

As a result of being increasingly positive and optimistic, you may also find yourself filled with a quiet calmness that comes with a heightened consciousness. People, strangers even, may be drawn to you and begin telling you their troubles, their ailments or their worries and concerns. This happens to me often, and I believe it is a blessing that comes with the responsibility for me to do less talking and more listening. Many times, people who are struggling simply want to know that they are being heard. As always, say a silent prayer to protect yourself, especially if you believe the individual to be under the influence of negative energy attachments. Also request to be infused with the wisdom of knowing how to articulate the very best response that will be for the greater good of the individual.

As you are doing your part to counteract and contradict spiritual warfare, you may also develop an interest in another facet of self-

UNDER SPIRITUAL SIEGE

discovery through discerning your spiritual gifts and talents. I alluded to this in chapter eight, and enacting the seven steps to spiritual wellness will prepare you tremendously for doing so. This is not a book about developing your psychic abilities, but it may inspire you to seek out those resources to aid you in doing so. Here is some fundamental information that you may find useful, not only in learning about yourself but in furthering your understanding of how good and negative energies communicate with us.

The five "clairs" are a good foundation from which to build your awareness: *clairvoyance*, *clairsentience*, *clairaudience*, *clairalience*, and *clairgustance*. These French words are spiritual aptitudes that, for the most part, correspond with our senses. You may recall that the "clair" prefix means "clear," pertaining to heightened clarity.

As I previously explained when telling my own story, clairvoyance, or "clear seeing," is the ability to receive visual information that one "sees" in his mind's eye. If you are already predisposed to being a highly visual person, chances are that you will also be clairvoyant, especially if imagining and picturing things in your head comes easily to you. A loving spiritual presence will communicate clairvoyantly by impressing visual inspirations within you or drawing your attention to visuals with which you have created an associative link in memory. But a negative energy would incite you with violent, harmful, frightening, or pornographic imagery that is not of your volition or intention.

Clairsentience, or "clear sensing," is a sensation of "knowingness" in the gut, commonly called "mother's intuition." It may very well have been clairsentience that swayed you in making a decision about a person, a place, or an opportunity, such as calling someone only to have them tell you they were just thinking of you in that very moment. When influenced by negative energy, clairsentience can make you feel nauseated or fearful. The fear then becomes the vehicle by which the negative energy gains power and control, influencing the person experiencing it to be filled with an increasing dread and self-doubt. This can lead to panic, which can lead to irrational, impulsive, or harmful choices in an effort to reduce or eradicate the unpleasant sensation as quickly as possible, instead of confronting it and exposing its manipulative tactics.

Next is clairaudience, which means "clear hearing." A loving spiritual presence might inspire you to hear music you would associate with something or someone special, or perhaps you'd hear a word, name, or sound that is relevant in a helpful way. For example, once during a psychic reading with a client, I kept hearing the song from *Mary Poppins* about a spoonful of sugar sweetly helping medicine to go down. I asked my client about it and she said her mother's name was Mary and that one of her fond and funny memories from childhood was of Mary chasing her through the house trying to get her to take her medicine! A negative energy using clairaudience would impose a repetitive "loop" of derogatory or defamatory language or self-deprecating thoughts, such as you have read from the people who are plagued with hearing unwanted voices.

As was previously discussed, a loving spiritual presence that appeals to your sense of "clear smelling," or clairalience, will send a fleeting waft of a scent that is nostalgic and reminiscent of a pleasant memory of a certain environment or someone in particular. The smell of roses has traditionally been associated with a profound religious or spiritual presence. A negative energy using clairalience will create a noxious odor that may compel you to think of tragic things such as a strong alcohol scent, the smell of rotting garbage, or the scent of fecal waste.

Like clairalience, clairgustance, or "clear tasting," is likely to be a momentary experience—just long enough for you to recognize it and make the proper association with it. A loving spiritual presence will create a brief taste on your tongue to prompt memories of a pleasant time. For example, you might taste chocolate chip cookie batter and immediately think of a departed grandmother because you recall how she always let you lick the spoon when she made cookies. But a negative energy will make you taste something strong and unpleasant such as alcohol, cigarettes, or blood in your mouth. In fact, once during a psychic gallery, I was channeling a very angry, spiteful man who was a ghost and had been a drug addict in his physical life. At one point, I was tasting blood in my mouth, and his family members responded by telling me that he had committed suicide by putting a gun in his mouth and pulling the trigger. I left him with some options to carefully consider and I'm happy to report that the next time I returned to that venue, his family also came back. This gentleman came forward in spirit and showed me such a remorseful yet positive attitude that I knew he had made the necessary transition and did so successfully.

The preceding are the primary spiritual gifts. You may experience one or more singly or in any number of combinations.

CHAPTER TEN

There are also adjunct spiritual gifts to the "clairs." You will also wish to be aware of these, especially if you are ready, willing, and able to counteract a spiritual siege. They are, in no particular order:

- ❖ TELEPATHY, WHICH IS THE MENTAL EXCHANGE OF THOUGHTS OR FEELINGS. THIS CAN ALSO OCCUR WITH ALL LIVING THINGS INCLUDING ANIMALS AND PLANTS. (AND REMEMBER THAT PRAYER IS ALSO TELEPATHY!)
- ❖ MEDIUMSHIP, WHICH IS THE ABILITY TO DISCERN AND COMMUNICATE WITH THE SOUL ENERGY OF SOMEONE WHO IS NO LONGER IN THE FLESH. THIS MAY ALSO INCLUDE ANIMALS.
- ❖ PSYCHOMETRY, WHICH IS THE ABILITY TO "READ," OR PERCEIVE INFORMATION, FROM AN OBJECT, SUCH AS A WATCH OR A PIECE OF JEWELRY SUCH AS A RING. OFTENTIMES, THE MOST VALUABLE AND ACCURATE INFORMATION COMES FROM OBJECTS THAT ARE METAL BECAUSE OF RETAINING THE ENERGY OF THE INDIVIDUAL WHO USED OR WORE THEM.
- ❖ MEDICAL INTUITIVE, WHICH IS THE ABILITY TO ROOT OUT AND IDENTIFY THE SOURCE OF SOMEONE'S PHYSICAL DISCOMFORT. THIS CAN ALSO OCCUR WITH ANIMALS. (IN FACT, I HAVE A DREAM THAT ONE DAY MEDICAL INTUITIVES WILL HAVE COMPLEMENTARY PRACTICES WITH PHYSICIANS, SURGEONS, AND VETERINARIANS.)
- ❖ HEALING, WHICH IS THE CAPACITY FOR RELIEVING OTHERS OF PAIN AND DISCOMFORT OR PERHAPS EVEN ACCELERATING THE HEALING PROCESS OF A WOUND. ONE VERSION OF HOW TO REMOVE NEGATIVE ENERGY FROM SOMEONE WAS EXPLAINED IN THE LAST CHAPTER. THERE ARE OTHER METHODS THAT YOU MAY WISH TO EXPLORE AND RESEARCH.
- ❖ AUTOMATIC WRITING (A FORM OF MEDIUMSHIP), WHICH IS THE ABILITY TO SERVE AS A CHANNEL THROUGH WHICH GLORIOUS, POSITIVE ENERGY FLOWS AND COMMUNICATES WHEN YOU PRESS A PEN TO PAPER.

As with all work of a spiritual nature, it is imperative to protect yourself in prayer, especially if you attempt mediumship or automatic writing. These modalities are very much about absolving control and allowing another force to step in and take the lead. People have similarly and unwittingly invited negative energies, including demons, into their households using similar modalities without the protection of prayer, such as when using Ouija boards. Engaging with "spirits" using a Ouija board for fun or entertainment is extremely dangerous if initiated by the inexperienced and without proper protection. It is, in essence, an open invitation for evil, negative, and predatory presences to swoop in and set up house in your living space. The most nefarious of them will masquerade as something they're not, such as a "lost" ghost child searching for his or her parents. It is akin to flinging open your front door and putting out a welcome mat for all ghosts and demons.

To the uninitiated, it is probably best to find someone whom you consider to be experienced, reputable, altruistic, and trustworthy to guide you in the exploration and authentic use of your spiritual gifts and talents. The only thing holding you back will be fear, which is precisely what the negative energies want—for you to doubt and second-guess your own abilities to the degree that you acquiesce, content yourself with mediocrity, and become ineffectual. Those fears tend to be:

◈ Fear of "bad" or prophetic information.
◈ Fear of the other party's response.
◈ Fear of being "wrong."
◈ Fear of losing control.

A good rule of thumb is to start low and go slow without rushing into anything. There is no cause for desperation or urgency no matter how impatient you are; allow it all to unfold in the time accorded to your evolution by the Universe and without force. If, on the other hand, everything is coming too hard and too fast, simply ask God or your Higher Power to put the brakes on, in the context of a prayer, of course. Your request will be accommodated.

I wish to share a story about my one and only experience with automatic writing that also takes into consideration the fears and doubts I had, similar to the preceding list. The outcome, however, was a truly remarkable and validating experience. In late December 2003, I pulled in too close to my mailbox and significantly scratched my car so much so that it needed repair work. It was one of those annoying instances that happened so quickly and yet magnified into a situation that would be time-consuming, inconvenient, and costly to resolve. Believing that everything happens for a reason, I struggled to make sense of precisely what I was intended to learn from the mishap (other than a caution about carelessness). It wasn't for nearly another month that the missing piece of the equation revealed itself so magnificently. See if you can follow the amazing domino effect that transpired.

I made arrangements to drop my car off at a body shop. Because of traveling, I was unable to schedule the work until January 19 and 20, days that I would be home and not in need of my vehicle. Knowing I would be homebound for two days, I stopped at the library a few weeks beforehand to get a couple of books to keep me company. In my ongoing spiritual research, I selected two. The first was a title I specifically had in mind while en route to the library, however the second book, *To Fly with the Angels*, was an afterthought. I saw it on the shelf behind me as I turned around to leave and was intrigued by the title.

Standing in line at the checkout, I turned over the *Angels* book and was pleasantly surprised to see that the authors were local, and that the book had been presented and inscribed to the library. I decided I would try contacting the authors at some future point.

I began my first book but, as the time drew closer to my car appointment, I switched books and became absorbed with *To Fly with the Angels*. The book was written by Charles Byrd, a man who had been a teacher and minister, and in it, he documents the most salient spiritual communications received by Mary Nell, his wife, over her lifetime. Beginning at a young age, Mary Nell discovered that she could receive spiritual messages in writing if she closed her eyes, touched a pen to paper, and waited for the pen to move of its own accord. This practice is commonly called, as noted earlier, "automatic writing." The messages Mary Nell has received are astoundingly profound, insightful, and of extraordinary spiritual elevation. Much of what has been communicated through her has been verified through the careful researching of facts.

On my second day home, I decided to place a phone call to the author in the hopes of arranging a sit-down meeting with him to discuss my own spiritual journey. He was listed in the local directory and lived minutes away. There was no answer, so I started to leave a recorded message when a woman interrupted the call, apologizing sweetly for not responding quickly enough. It was Mary Nell. Her voice was gentle and loving, lilting with an inborn sense of joy and tinged with a faint Southern drawl.

After a moment of dialogue, during which I spoke of her husband's book, her voice broke as she told me that he had passed the previous October after a long illness. She confessed that it had been extremely difficult for her to cope with his loss; they had been inordinately close and shared a long and loving courtship that lasted many years. She was now struggling, confronted with a void such as she had never before imagined. In spite of the affirmations offered by her faith, she now felt alone and lonely though her time was filled with comforting friends and minding her young grandchildren. She welcomed my call but suggested we meet at another time, sometime after she felt ready and well enough (though she didn't sound optimistic). I thanked her for being so gracious and we parted ways.

I went back to reading *Angels* but, after my conversation with Mary Nell, I was feeling nudged and prodded to try automatic writing. I shrugged it off, but still I felt compelled by something persistent. I was well aware of the concept and had even witnessed it firsthand once before. It was not something especially interesting to me, nor was I intrigued enough to make it part of my repertoire. To be successful, a portion of one's will must be absolved, given over and trusting of Spirit to control the manual scripting of ink on paper. I'd never been one to forfeit control but, in the moment, I sensed this was something I must attempt.

I returned to the stool where I had placed my call to Mary Nell and seated myself with a legal pad and the same pen I used to jot down information during our earlier conversation. In my left hand, I held my blessed cross and, before beginning, I said a prayer in which I requested that only pure and positive energy be permitted to come forth. I next closed my eyes so as not to be visually influenced by the process. Then I waited. After a moment or two, I had the sensation of the pen moving out from under me, slowly scrolling along the surface of the pad. Gooseflesh raised along my skin but I quieted my fears by remaining focused and altruistic; this allowed the anxiety to subside. Still, an electrical tingling remained. The pen had stopped and I silently reinforced to the presence that this was a two-way street: I was trusting just as I expected to be trusted in return. The pen continued its downward path, looping and weaving until it ceased. I opened my eyes and looked. There were several words and all but the first were linked in a single line of ink that never left the paper. It spelled, "Mary Nell requires _____"— although Nell was spelled "N-l-l," and "requires" was missing its "i." The last word was one I could not discern though it seemed to have four letters. The otherworldly calligraphy then drifted into a curling, curving doodle of sorts before coming to a stop.

I thought, at first, that the odd word might be "love" but that didn't make sense: "Mary Nell requires *love*." Even given my brief conversation with her, I was certain that more than a few loving friends

UNDER SPIRITUAL SIEGE

and family members surrounded her. So, I did the only logical thing and openly requested clarification of the illegible word. I pressed my pen to the paper and waited. It came quickly enough and with legible determination: "rose." "Mary Nell requires *rose*" was the complete message. In fact, when revisiting the "doodle," it now, of course, resembled a rose with a central bud and blossoming petals.

I wasn't certain of what it meant, though I knew I had given psychic readings in which people had been the recipients of roses from loved ones who had passed on. In one instance, I saw a woman's mother lay a bouquet of pink—not red—roses in the woman's lap; she immediately affirmed pink roses were her favorite flower. I also thought the word "requires" unusual. It seemed to connote a timeliness or urgency. Still, I was not about to contact Mary Nell, a lovely woman but essentially a stranger, in order to say, "I think I have a message for you" without something more tangible and concrete.

A short while later I continued to internally debate this very issue. Feeling some exasperation, I picked up the *Angels* book and carried it to the family room where I plopped down on the sofa with the book in my lap. But instead of reading again, I clicked on the television and began random channel surfing. When I jumped to the *third* station (I associate the number three with the Holy Trinity) a movie was playing, the title of which, displayed momentarily on the screen, grabbed my immediate attention. It was 1968's *The Subject was Roses* and as I watched, the scene that played out before me was one in which a husband gives his wife a bouquet of roses for which she is overjoyed to receive. That did it—there was my reinforcement, my validation; *and* I had the *Angels* book right there in my lap. I decided I would try calling Mary Nell the next day and determine a tactful way to tell her of my experience.

The following morning I called Mary Nell, but there was no answer so I left a cautious, carefully worded message. I told her I wished to share with her something "out of the ordinary" that transpired after she and I had spoken the day before. The call went unreturned and all day long I wondered and worried if I had done the right thing. After all, I was a stranger and I certainly didn't wish my actions to be misinterpreted as harmful, hurtful or delusional. But shortly after 6:00 p.m. that evening, Mary Nell called back, having been away from home for the day.

I slowly related to her all that had happened as carefully and respectfully as I could, pausing to gauge her comfort level (she provided assurances throughout). Finally, after giving her the message, "Mary Nell requires rose," I asked her if receiving a rose or roses meant anything to her. There was a moment of silence. Then she wept and said that, yes, it did. Mary Nell related that whenever her husband Charles would go out anywhere, he never failed to return without a single yellow rose—her favorite. She only ever wished for one rose, as she felt a bouquet detracted from the beauty of each individual flower.

She was joyous and relieved! Close friends had provided her with "visions" of her husband but nothing nearly as specific as this! It was the moment she had been awaiting and she now felt uplifted. In fact, she confided something she had told no one else: in her struggle to assimilate to widowed life, she had secretly believed she would receive a sign from her husband within three months of his passing. Through divine grace, the message for Mary Nell had come *exactly* three months to the day after his passing.

There will also be occasions in your spiritual growth and development when you feel "blocked up" by low energy and unable to "connect" to your gifts properly. This is all part of the process, and is God's way of helping you to pace yourself. It is temporary, and you will recover and bounce back in short order, which will be in a time frame unique to each individual.

UNDER SPIRITUAL SIEGE

CONCLUSION

This book was intended as a primer, or very basic beginning guide, to understanding how to differentiate between spiritual presences that are loving and supportive and those that are ill-intended and destructive. Hopefully, this is all much clearer now and you may wish to explore other books on these topics to further your understanding.

More importantly, this book was also intended to serve as a resource to create a personal awareness of the spiritual tools available and accessible to you in any given moment. In so doing, you have extraordinary potential to feel confident, resilient, and empowered to resist the temptation and deceptive seduction of negative energies such as ghosts and demons. The spiritual siege under which we are presently embattled is likely to continue for some time to come. Which faction you side with is a choice. Elect to serve on the side of the "Light Brigade Cavalry" in order to diffuse and disarm parasitic, negative energies. What you have to contribute is of the greatest value of the highest order, and *you* are very much needed to aid in fighting the good fight. See you there!

Photo by Gary Edmiston

ABOUT THE AUTHOR

Psychic **William Stillman** is the internationally known, award-winning author of the *Autism and the God Connection* book trilogy, which explores aspects of spiritual giftedness in many people with autism. These books encompass *Autism and the God Connection*, *The Soul of Autism*, and *The Autism Prophecies*. He is also the author of the book *Conversations with Dogs: A Psychic Reveals What Our Canine Companions Have to Say (And How You Can Talk to Them Too!)*.

Since 2004, Stillman has worked professionally as a psychic and spiritual counselor at Alta View Wellness Center in Harrisburg, Pennsylvania (www.altaviewwellness.com). His accuracy in discerning the truth and making predictions that come to fruition has been acclaimed by his clients as truly extraordinary. He specializes in identifying clients' gifts and talents as well as aiding discarnate spirits (ghosts) to transition to the Heavenly realm. Stillman has also relieved others of the physical symptoms of pain and discomfort using prayer. Stillman does not consider himself to be a medium, although he regularly connects with loved ones who have crossed over. He has been consulted on missing person and unsolved homicide cases.

Stillman has been interviewed on numerous radio shows of a paranormal nature, including *Coast to Coast AM*, the most listened to overnight radio program in North America. He has been interviewed on the Web series *CharVision* by internationally renowned psychic medium Char Margolis, who called Stillman "really fascinating," and he has been a guest on the popular YouTube series *Swedenborg and Life*.

Stillman has twice been a guest speaker for Lily Dale Assembly, near Jamestown, New York, the country's oldest spiritualist community. He also teaches a class titled "Developing Your Personal Intuition," Levels I and II, among others. Stillman firmly believes that we all possess psychic gifts to be developed and employed to be of service to others.

Above all, William Stillman especially enjoys facilitating psychic group galleries (similar to John Edward on TV's *Crossing Over*), and he treasures the amazing opportunities and validations that have come from touring his galleries throughout Pennsylvania and beyond.

Find out more about him at his personal website:
www.williamstillman.com.

Devils and Demonology: In the 21st Century. Katie Boyd. Occultism, exorcism, and demonic entities are in cultures around the world. Learn what to look for if you are a paranormal investigator and what you can do ensure you are never a victim. Read cases, of people helped by a demonologist. Remember, what you can see in this world can hurt you, but what you can't, can kill you.
Size: 6" x 9" • 17 b/w photos & ills. • 160 pp. ISBN: 978-0-7643-3195-4 • soft cover • $14.99

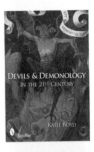

Exorcism: How to Clear a Spirit-Possessed Person. Eugene Maurey. Exorcism of a spirit performed at a distance.
Size: 6" x 9" • 176 pp.
ISBN: 978-0-914918-88-2 • soft cover • $14.99

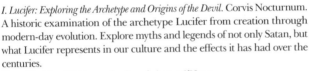

I. Lucifer: Exploring the Archetype and Origins of the Devil. Corvis Nocturnum. A historic examination of the archetype Lucifer from creation through modern-day evolution. Explore myths and legends of not only Satan, but what Lucifer represents in our culture and the effects it has had over the centuries.
Size: 6" x 9" • 76 b/w and color photos • 176 pp.
ISBN: 978-0-7643-3919-6 • soft cover • $19.99

Afterlife: What Really Happens on the Other Side: True Stories of Contact and Communication with Spirits. Barry R. Strohm. Delve into the mysteries of earth-bound ghosts, reincarnation, heaven, hell, messages from spirit guides, the concept of preordained events, and much more. As the author and a clairvoyant explore afterlife communication, find out what those on the other side have to say.
Size: 6" x 9" • 46 b/w images • 160 pp.
ISBN: 978-0-7643-4734-4 • soft cover • $16.99

Schiffer Publishing, Ltd.
4880 Lower Valley Rd.,
Atglen, PA 19310
Phone (610) 593-1777, Fax (610) 593-2002
E-mail: Info@schifferbooks.com

Printed in China

Schiffer books may be ordered from your local bookstore, or they may be ordered directly from the publisher.

Please visit our web site catalog at
www.schifferbooks.com
or write for a free catalog.